The Utah Adventure

History of a Centennial State

John McCormick

Revised Edition

SALT LAKE CITY

08 07 06 05 04 03   13 12 11 10 9 8

Published by
Gibbs Smith, Publisher
P.O. Box 667
Layton UT 84041
(800) 748-5439
text@gibbs-smith.com
www.gibbs-smith.com/textbooks

Senior editor, Susan Allen Myers

Also edited by Nikki Hansen

Book design by Kathleen Timmerman

Cover photo by Tom Till

Original art by Gary Rasmussen

Maps by Alaine Sweet

Printed and bound in Malaysia

Advisors/Reviewers

Nancy N. Mathews, Past State Social Studies Specialist, Utah State Office of Education

Kim Hadfield, Past Social Studies Coordinator, Davis School District

Norma Jean Remington, Social Studies Curriculum Director K-12, Davis School District

Maria Peterson, Fine Arts, Salt Lake City School District

James Johnson, Assisstant Superintendent, Washington School District

Dennis Duffey, Director of Elementary Education, Alpine School District

Richard Sadler, Professor of History, Weber State University

Forrest Cuch, Director, Utah State Division of Indian Affairs

Mark Maryboy, Navajo Nation and San Juan County Commission

Ronald J. Gardner, Government Consultant, Disability Law Center

ISBN 0-87905-719-X

UTAH

Utah's State Seal

The American eagle means protection in peace and war. The beehive stands for industry, or hard work. The American flag tells of Utah's allegiance to the United States of America. The sego lilies are Utah's state flowers. 1847—the year the pioneers first came into the Salt Lake Valley. 1896—the year Utah became a state.

Utah State Motto: Industry

The beehive is an emblem of industry and hard work.

Contents

Maps and Charts

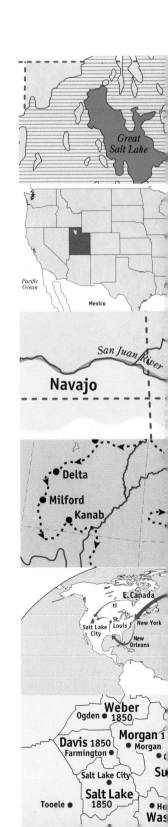

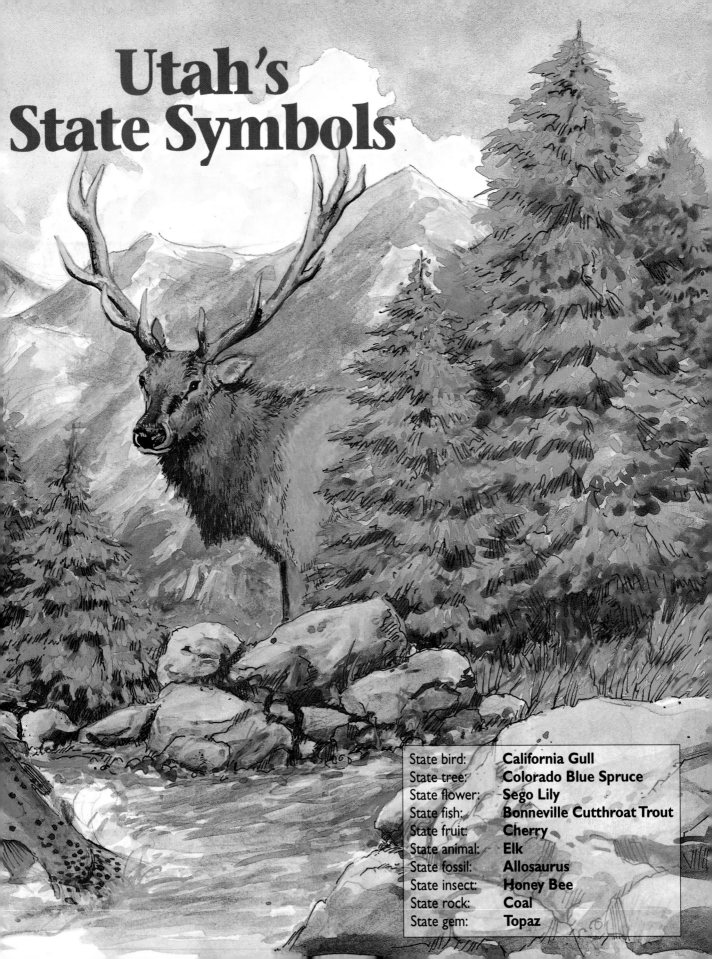

Utah's State Symbols

State bird:	California Gull
State tree:	Colorado Blue Spruce
State flower:	Sego Lily
State fish:	Bonneville Cutthroat Trout
State fruit:	Cherry
State animal:	Elk
State fossil:	Allosaurus
State insect:	Honey Bee
State rock:	Coal
State gem:	Topaz

Dinosaur tracks!
Some of the largest tracks
in North America are at
Hurricane Cliffs, Utah.

Natural Utah

Utah seems very large to us. Yet it is just one small part of the world. Because we live in Utah, it is important to us. It is our home. Millions of people all over the world live in places important to them. In this chapter you will begin to learn about Utah by studying its **geography**. Geography is the land, plants, people and animals of a place. First we will study where Utah is located in the world. We will learn what Utah's land is like, and how it got that way. We will see how people in Utah are connected with people all over the world.

Why is it important to know about the geography of a place? Because geography affects where we live and how we live.

For example, more people live on flat land than in mountains. Flat land is easier to build homes on, and it is easier to farm.

In some places in the world, rain waters all the crops. Not here! In order to farm in Utah, people settle on flat land where water flows from mountain streams. They dig ditches to bring water from lakes and streams to their farms. They plant crops that do not need much water, such as special kinds of wheat. This is called dry farming. People's lives in Utah are affected by the geography of the dry place where they live.

Here are some examples of geography in the lives of people who lived here long ago.

The first people to live here were hunters and gatherers. (We will talk more about them in the next chapter.) To find

Porcupines live in Utah. They are part of our geography.

"The world has seemed more beautiful to me than ever before. . . . I have seemed to be at one with the world. . . . In the meantime, my burro and I, and a little dog, if I can find one, are going on and on, until, sooner or later, we reach the end of the horizon."
—*Everett Ruess, 1931*

food, the men, women, and children traveled on foot all over the state. They hunted wild animals. They gathered nuts, berries, and roots from wild plants. It is often too dry for plants to grow here, so the people could not find enough plants and berries in one place. They had to travel around looking for them.

Much later, another group of people, the Utes, lived near Utah Lake. There was enough food where they lived. At the lake they could catch delicious fish and ducks, and they could find smooth, round duck eggs to eat. In the mountains nearby, they could gather acorns, and hunt deer. Unlike the first people, the Utes did not have to move around much to find food to eat.

Utes lived near Utah Lake and the mountains, where it was easy to get wood and water, and animals for food.

Location: Where in the World Are We?

We all know we live on the planet Earth. What else do you know about where we live? Utah is located on one of the world's **continents**. Continents are very large land areas. They have oceans on many sides.

Utah is part of a country on the North American continent. A country is a land region under the control of one government. Our country is the United States of America. There is a country on the north and another country on the south of our country. Which countries are they?

Utah's Place in the World

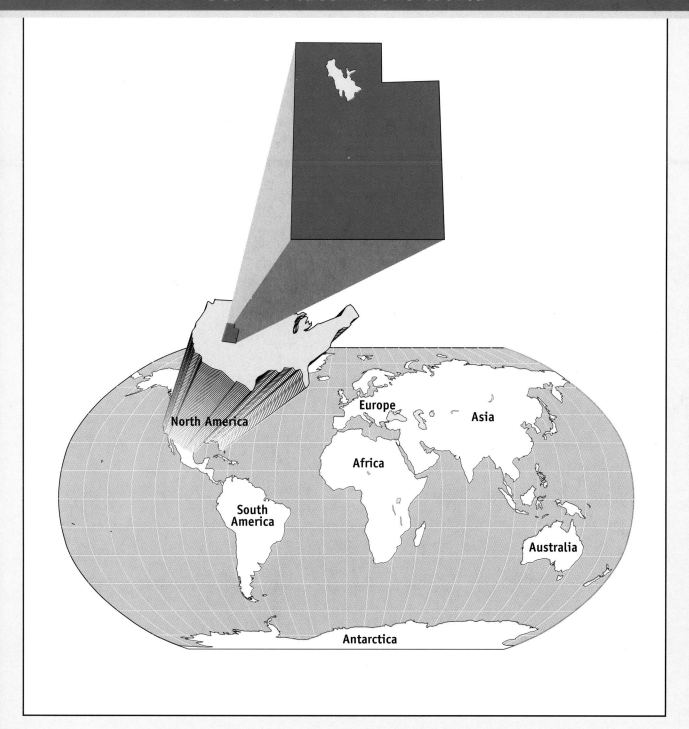

North America

Europe

Asia

Africa

South
America

Australia

Antarctica

Utah in the United States

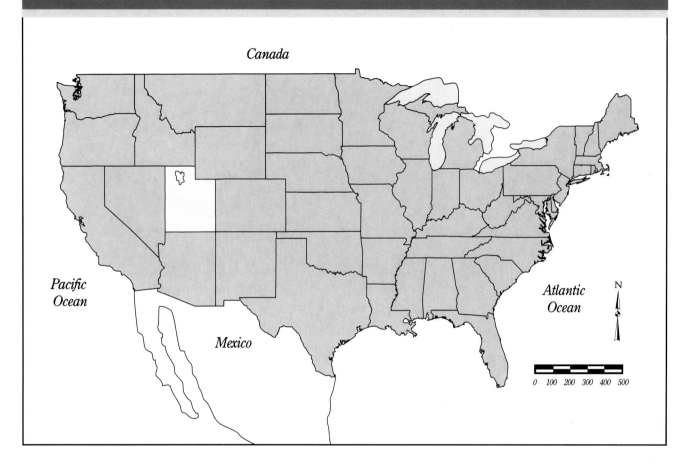

Our country is divided up into fifty parts called states. Utah is one of the states in the United States. Each state has other divisions, which are often called counties. The town, city, or farm where you live is found in a county.

So, there you have it:

city, town, or farm ➠county ➠state ➠country ➠continent ➠planet

Regions

A region is another way to tell where we are. Regions organize places that are alike in some way.

You can live in many regions all at the same time. We live in the West. This means that we are one of the many states in the large western region of the United States.

There are mining regions, where there are lots of gold, silver, or copper mines. You might live in a farming region and watch the corn grow taller than you are each summer.

Even schools are organized into regions known as districts. What school district do you live in?

Landforms

A landform is a feature of the earth's surface. Three main kinds of landforms are found in Utah—mountains, plateaus, and basins. All of these are the result of powerful forces moving inside the earth. They are also the result of wind and water wearing away the earth's surface. This is called **erosion**.

Mountains are very high land formations. A hill is like a mountain, but it is not as high.

Basins are very large, low, flat areas of land that are surrounded by mountains or high plateaus. They are shaped like huge bowls.

Valleys are much smaller basins found between two mountain areas.

Plateaus are high, wide, flat areas that often end with steep cliffs or mountains. They look like tables or wide steps many miles across. Sometimes they are called "table lands."

Wind and water often cut deep canyons or strange shapes into plateaus.

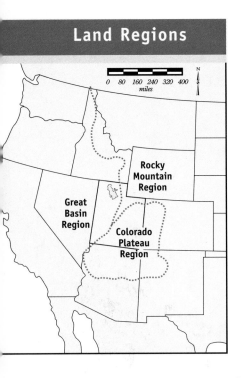

Landform Regions

Utah is divided into three land regions. Each land region has mostly one type of landform, such as mountains, plateaus, or basins. The three main land regions in Utah are the Rocky Mountain region, the Colorado Plateau region, and the Great Basin region.

The Rocky Mountain Region

The mountains in this region are beautiful to look at. Most of them are covered with forests. Many animals live in the forests. People use the wood from forest trees. They hike and camp in the cool mountains. Mountains are also important for storing snow in winter. The snow melts in the spring and runs into streams. The streams flow into rivers, lakes, and reservoirs. This is how the snow provides water for people who live in valleys.

Do you wonder how these mountains were formed? Have you wondered how long they have been here? They are very old. Scientists think they were formed millions of years ago. The youngest mountains have tall, jagged peaks. Mountains that are older are more rounded, because the wind and rain have worn them away. This is a type of erosion.

Most of the mountains in Utah were formed by forces inside the earth that caused huge blocks of land to squeeze into

Utahns are lucky to have such beautiful mountains. There is a lot more snow and rain in the mountains than in the valleys. The water runs down the streams and is used by the people who live in the valleys below.

Photo by Jeannie Young ▲

each other from opposite directions. This caused some parts of the land to rise up, and even fold over on top of each other.

Some of Utah's mountains were formed by forces inside the earth that pushed up the land from underneath. The Henry and LaSal Mountains were formed this way.

Another way mountains were formed was by volcanoes. The inside of the earth is made of rock so hot it has melted and become liquid. When it is inside the earth, it is called magma. In some places forces deep inside the earth push the magma up through the crust of the earth to the outside. Once magma pours out onto the earth's surface, it is called lava. Lava is ten times hotter than boiling water. When lava gets

A volcanic cone near Fillmore is in the Black Rock Desert.

into the air, it cools and becomes hard. If a volcano keeps erupting, layers of lava build up around it to form a mountain.

A volcano that erupts often is called an active volcano. A volcano that is quiet for many years is called a dormant (or sleeping) volcano. If scientists think it will never erupt again, it is called an **extinct** (or dead) volcano.

Volcanoes are found all over the world. Utah has extinct volcanoes near Fillmore in the Black Rock Desert and north of Santa Clara.

Pressure inside the earth also makes geysers, hot springs, and boiling mud pools. Inside the earth, water gets very hot. Sometimes it shoots up through the earth's crust and into the air. Fountains of hot water and steam are called geysers. There are no active geysers in Utah today. Hot springs form when the hot water flows out of the ground. They are found throughout Utah. One, called Iron Springs, is near Ogden. There are also hot springs in Salt Lake City, Castilla, Grantsville, Lehi, the Sevier Desert, Midway, Monroe, Milford, and near the Virgin River.

Strike It Rich!

Did you know there is a rich supply of silver, gold, copper, and other minerals in Utah mountains?

You use copper more than you might think. If you have electric wires, a television set, or a computer, then you use copper! A lot of the coins in your bank are made of copper. Silver and gold are used for rings and other jewelry but they are used in other important ways, too. Do some research to learn more about Utah's minerals.

"If there is magic on this earth it lies in water, and nowhere is water so beautiful as in the desert, for nowhere else is it so scarce. . . . In the desert each drop is precious."

—*Edward Abbey*

▲ Gila Monster
▼ Desert Tortoise

▲ Prairie Dog

The Great Basin Region

Another large land region is the Great Basin. Most of the area is hot and dry. It is one of the driest deserts in the United States. Even though it has a desert climate, the Great Salt Lake and Utah Lake are in this region. Mountain streams run into them. There are some mountains in the Great Basin, too. But it is mostly flat, like the bottom of a smooth bowl.

Most of Utah's people live in the Great Basin. Why would they live in such a dry desert? They live on the edges of the basin near the mountains. Here the land is flat, which makes good places for cities and farms. It is near the mountains, whose streams supply water.

In some places the deserts seem so hot and dry you wonder if anything could live there. But desert animals and plants do live in the Great Basin. The desert tortoise moves slowly across the sand. Prairie dogs dig holes and burrow underneath the ground, where it is much cooler. Both of these animals are protected by laws because they are in danger of becoming extinct. Lizards, snakes, and insects like to hide between rocks and under plants in the desert.

Sagebrush and cactus, salt and sand are common in the Great Basin.

Ancient Lake Bonneville

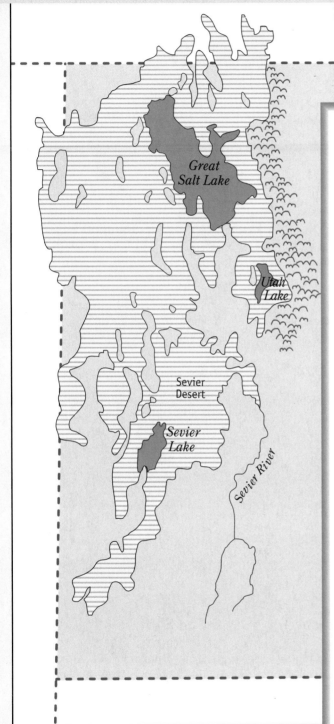

Map Key

⬡ Lake Bonneville
⬛ Today's lakes

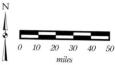

N

0 10 20 30 40 50
miles

The natural regions of Utah have not always been the way they are now. Utah used to be a lot different. It is still changing. It will always change.

Long, long, ago, the weather in Utah was much colder than it is now. Because it was so cold, big masses of snow and ice formed in the mountains. These are called **glaciers**. The snow and ice just kept piling up. Long, thick layers covered the ground. Then slowly the glaciers began to move. They crept downhill and took a lot of the dirt and rock with them. They wore away the land, and carved many canyons and valleys in Utah's mountains. One of these is Little Cottonwood Canyon, southeast of Salt Lake City.

Then the weather began to change and slowly get warmer. The ice began to melt. Water from the melting glaciers ran down the canyons and into a growing lake. The lake spread over the flat land of the Great Basin and through canyons and mountain valleys. Cache Valley and Heber Valley were also full of water.

The ancient lake washed up against the Wasatch Mountains and made a bench. You can still see it on the mountains today. The line shows how high the water reached. Eventually the lake covered much of Utah. Then, after a long time, the water cut a new huge river that drained all the way to the Pacific Ocean. When explorers came to the area thousands of years later, they called the old lake Lake Bonneville. The Great Salt Lake, Utah Lake, and Sevier Lake are all that is left of that ancient lake today.

Photo by Kelly Ross

A Salty Lake

Even though the Great Basin is a desert, Utah's largest body of water is located in it. It is called the Great Salt Lake. Three major rivers and many small streams flow into the lake. These rivers carry in salt and other minerals. But there are no rivers to carry the salt out. That is why the lake is so salty. It is saltier than any of the oceans. It is so salty that no fish can live in it—only small brine shrimp.

Explorers who found the lake, like Jim Bridger, thought it was part of the Pacific Ocean. For a long time, the first maps showed a lake in Utah called "Lake Timpanogas" with a river running all the way from it to the Pacific Ocean. Men traveled in a boat all around the lake and learned that it was not connected to the ocean.

The Great Salt Lake has always been important to people in Utah. Native Americans lived near the lake to catch the ducks and birds that nest along its shores. When pioneers first reached the Salt Lake Valley, they traveled to the lake to get salt. Salt mining and brine shrimp harvesting still go on today. Later amusement parks and resorts were built on its shores—the most famous one was named Saltair. The Great Salt Lake is famous around the world.

The Colorado Plateau Region

Another of Utah's large land regions is the Colorado Plateau. It is a broad space of high land that is hard and rocky. Some of Utah's most beautiful scenery is found in this region. Over millions of years wind and rain have carved wonderful rock formations. Colorful cliffs rise a thousand feet above the valley floor and stretch as far as a hundred miles. All five of Utah's national parks are in the Colorado Plateau. People come from all over the world to visit them.

Two mighty rivers have cut deep and beautiful canyons through this region. They are the Colorado River and the Green River. They are the only major rivers in Utah that go all the way to an ocean.

Photo by Tom Till ▶

At Dead Horse Point State Park you can see the Colorado River winding through sandstone cliffs.

Sedimentary Rock

The Colorado Plateau is made up of layers of rock called **sedimentary** rock.

For a long time most of Utah was underwater. Shallow seas covered it. Rivers flowed into the seas, carrying sand, mud, and small pebbles. These things are called **sediments**. All of this material then settled on the bottom of the seas in many layers. When the seas dried up, the area became dry land. Then, for thousands of years, winds blew hundreds of feet of sand onto the rock layers and formed the bright red colors of the cliffs we see today.

Under the Ground

Coal, oil, and natural gas are an underground treasure in our state. They provide heat for our homes and energy to run engines. Without them we could not run our cars and trucks. Today most of Utah's electricity is produced by generators powered by burning coal. Important minerals are also part of the treasure. Be a detective and find out what minerals are in our rocks and dirt.

Utah's Parks and Monuments

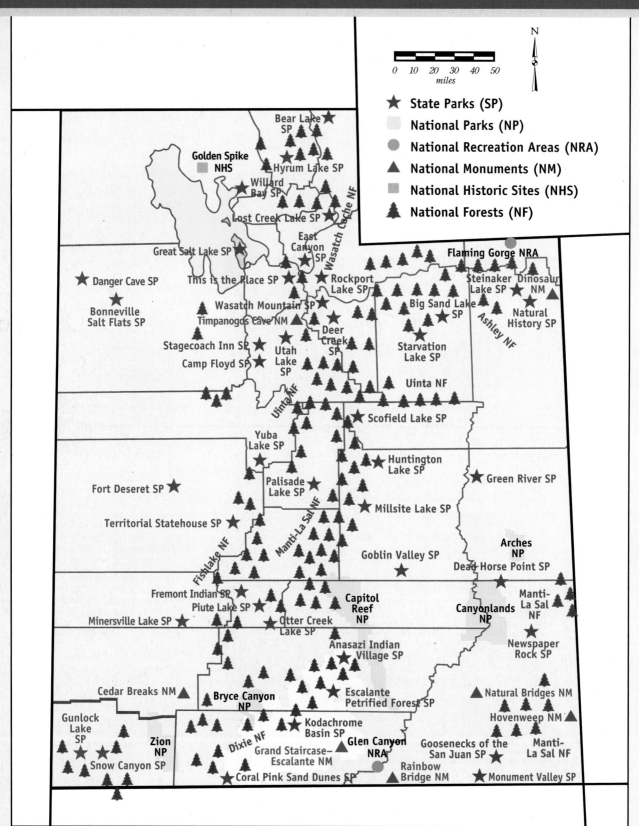

Legend:
- ★ State Parks (SP)
- National Parks (NP)
- ● National Recreation Areas (NRA)
- ▲ National Monuments (NM)
- ■ National Historic Sites (NHS)
- 🌲 National Forests (NF)

0 10 20 30 40 50 miles

N

Bear Lake SP
Golden Spike NHS
Hyrum Lake SP
Willard Bay SP
Lost Creek Lake SP
East Canyon SP
Great Salt Lake SP
Wasatch Cache NF
Danger Cave SP
This is the Place SP
Rockport Lake SP
Flaming Gorge NRA
Steinaker Lake SP
Dinosaur NM
Bonneville Salt Flats SP
Wasatch Mountain SP
Big Sand Lake SP
Natural History SP
Ashley NF
Timpanogos Cave NM
Deer Creek SP
Stagecoach Inn SP
Utah Lake SP
Starvation Lake SP
Camp Floyd SP
Uinta NF
Scofield Lake SP
Uinta NF
Yuba Lake SP
Huntington Lake SP
Green River SP
Fort Deseret SP
Palisade Lake SP
Millsite Lake SP
Territorial Statehouse SP
Manti-La Sal NF
Fishlake NF
Goblin Valley SP
Arches NP
Dead Horse Point SP
Fremont Indian SP
Piute Lake SP
Capitol Reef NP
Canyonlands NP
Manti-La Sal NF
Minersville Lake SP
Otter Creek Lake SP
Newspaper Rock SP
Anasazi Indian Village SP
Cedar Breaks NM
Bryce Canyon NP
Escalante Petrified Forest SP
Natural Bridges NM
Gunlock Lake SP
Hovenweep NM
Zion NP
Kodachrome Basin SP
Dixie NF
Grand Staircase–Escalante NM
Glen Canyon NRA
Goosenecks of the San Juan SP
Manti-La Sal NF
Snow Canyon SP
Coral Pink Sand Dunes SP
Rainbow Bridge NM
Monument Valley SP

Bryce Canyon National Park and Arches National Park photos by John George ▶ Zion National Park, Canyonlands National Park, and Capitol Reef photos by Tom Till

Utah's National Parks

Many places in Utah are unusual and beautiful. They have been made into national and state parks and monuments. The government pays park rangers to take care of them.

Zion National Park was Utah's first national park, named in 1919. Over thousands of years the Virgin River flowed down through the rock and cut beautiful canyons. The first people to live there were an American Indian group called the Anasazi. Later Southern Paiute Indians moved in. They were living there when the Mormon pioneers arrived in Utah.

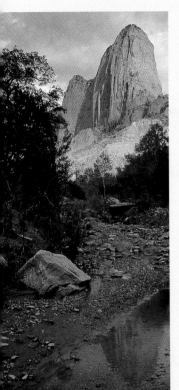

▲ Zion National Park

▼ Bryce Canyon National Park

Bryce Canyon National Park is the most colorful park in the world. White, yellow, red, orange, and purple rocks blend together. Wind, ice, and water carved the rocks in Bryce Canyon into all kinds of shapes. The park was named after Ebenezer Bryce, an early rancher in the area. Once he looked into the deep canyon and said this was no place to lose a cow!

Arches National Park is named for its many stone arches. The rocks are mainly pink sandstone. A stream of water can wear a hole in this kind of rock. Blowing sand can also wear a hole through the rock. This happens slowly. It takes thousands and thousands of years. It is still going on. American Indians long ago lived among the arches. They made a lot of rock art there. The figures on the rock look like they might be bighorn sheep.

▲ Arches National Park

Canyonlands National Park is the largest of Utah's parks. It has deep gorges and huge rock towers. The state's three major rivers run through it—the Green River, the Colorado River, and the San Juan River. Fremont people hunted in Canyonlands. Later the Anasazi farmed there. There are many ruins and rock art from these people.

Capitol Reef National Park has beautiful, red sandstone cliffs with strange rock formations. They were made by water cutting into them. Rock art shows us that American Indians lived there for many years. Butch Cassidy and the Sundance Kid used Capitol Reef as a hideout.

▲ Canyonlands National Park

▼ Capitol Reef National Park

Native Americans had a name for Bryce Canyon. It meant "red rocks standing like men in a bowl-shaped canyon."

**Animals that lived here
10,000 years ago are now extinct.**
(Photo of panorama by Helga Teiwes)

Ancient Animals

While Utah's land was being formed, many animals also lived here. Many of these animals have become extinct. They no longer live anywhere on Earth. When they died, their bones sometimes became part of the layers of sediment. They became **petrified** and turned to rock. Bones of many animals have been found in Utah: musk oxen, horses, camels, deer, mountain lions, woolly mammoths, and even dinosaurs.

People have been finding dinosaur **fossils** here for at least a hundred years. Fossils are hardened bones, or shapes of plants and animals in rock. Most of the dinosaur bones dug up in Utah have come from the Allosaurus. Other plant and meat eaters have also been uncovered, and parts of dinosaur egg shells have been found. Giant dinosaur footprints are still found in rocks around Utah.

Allosaurus is Utah's state fossil.

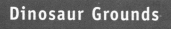

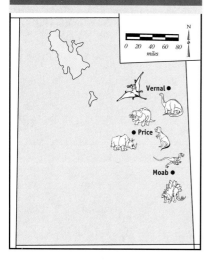

Dinosaur Grounds

0 20 40 60 80
miles

N

Vernal ●

● Price

Moab ●

Scientists study huge dinosaur bones at Dinosaur National Monument.

Altogether, more than three hundred dinosaur skeletons have been uncovered in Utah. There are many pits, or quarries, in Utah. Scientists called **paleontologists** continue to find dinosaur skeletons in them. The two best-known quarries are the Cleveland-Lloyd Dinosaur Quarry near Price, and the quarry at Dinosaur National Monument near Vernal. Ogden has a Dinosaur Park with over thirty life-sized models that can help you imagine what it might have been like to live in dinosaur days.

Utah's Animals Today

When you wake up in the morning, listen to the birds singing outside. Hundreds of different kinds of birds live in Utah. Some of them stay here all the time. Others just stop for a short time to rest, feed, and breed, on their yearly flights from Canada to Mexico and back again. Many kinds of ducks and other water birds also live near the rivers and lakes. We don't have an ocean, but we do have white pelicans and seagulls.

Many birds in Utah are birds of prey, called raptors. That means they swoop down, catch small animals in their beaks and claws, and take them to a safe place to eat them. The golden eagle is the largest raptor. Many bald eagles spend the winter and early spring here every year. There are also many hawks and owls.

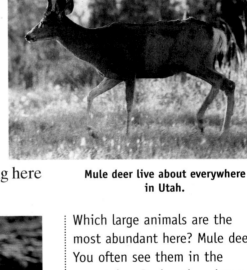

Mule deer live about everywhere in Utah.

The golden eagle, Utah's largest raptor, nests high on a sandstone cliff.

This mountain lion lives in the mountains of southern Utah.

Which large animals are the most abundant here? Mule deer! You often see them in the mountains. During the winter, when they are looking for food, you may see them in your yard! One man said the deer came during the night and ate the apples off his trees, then they ate some branches off the trees. He liked the beautiful deer so much he didn't mind.

18

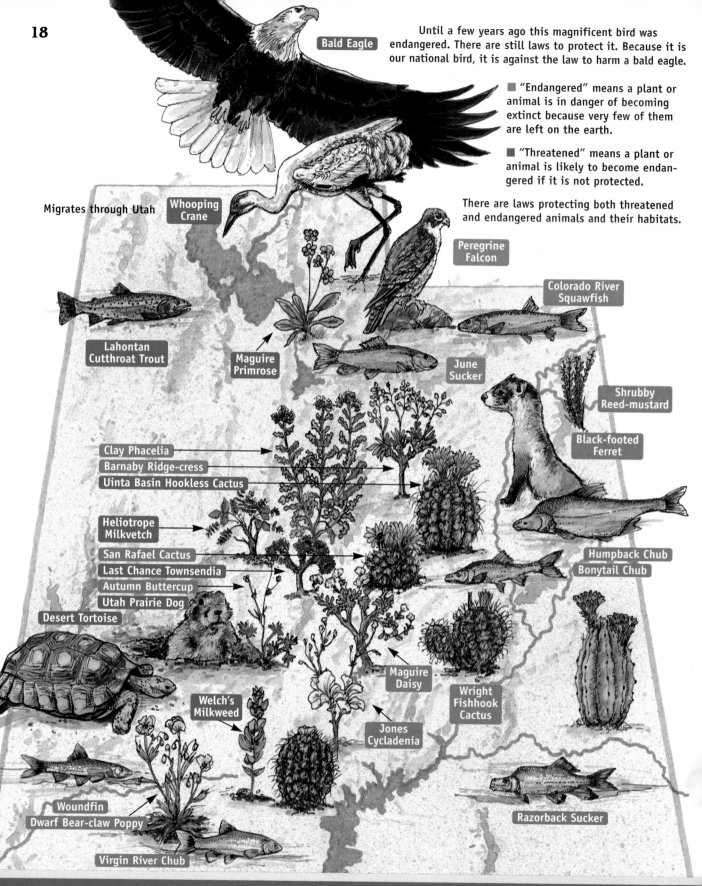

Until a few years ago this magnificent bird was endangered. There are still laws to protect it. Because it is our national bird, it is against the law to harm a bald eagle.

Bald Eagle

■ "Endangered" means a plant or animal is in danger of becoming extinct because very few of them are left on the earth.

■ "Threatened" means a plant or animal is likely to become endangered if it is not protected.

There are laws protecting both threatened and endangered animals and their habitats.

Migrates through Utah

Whooping Crane

Peregrine Falcon

Colorado River Squawfish

Lahontan Cutthroat Trout

Maguire Primrose

June Sucker

Shrubby Reed-mustard

Black-footed Ferret

Clay Phacelia
Barnaby Ridge-cress
Uinta Basin Hookless Cactus

Heliotrope Milkvetch

San Rafael Cactus
Last Chance Townsendia
Autumn Buttercup
Utah Prairie Dog

Humpback Chub
Bonytail Chub

Desert Tortoise

Maguire Daisy

Wright Fishhook Cactus

Welch's Milkweed

Jones Cycladenia

Woundfin
Dwarf Bear-claw Poppy

Razorback Sucker

Virgin River Chub

Utah's Threatened and Endangered Species

Majestic moose, elk, and antelope wander in the mountains and valleys. Watch out! Utah also has bobcats, cougars, and black bears. We have fur-bearing animals like weasels, raccoons, muskrats, badgers, foxes, and jack rabbits. Ever smelled a skunk? They usually hide from people, but they are there.

Beavers were once nearly extinct here. Fur trappers got most of them when felt hats were popular (we will study the trappers in Chapter 4). Lots of beavers now live near our mountain lakes.

Have you ever slept in a sleeping bag in the mountains, crept out of a tent just as the sun was coming up, and gone fishing? Did you catch a trout? The cutthroat trout is our state fish. It is **indigenous** to Utah. That means it was here naturally, even before people came. No one brought it here. Later, people brought other fish from other places to live in our lakes and streams.

Utah's Plants

Plants are an important part of Utah's natural environment. Some kinds are found all over the state. Others grow only in certain regions where the climate suits them better.

People use plants in many ways. Some are indigenous to Utah and others are not. The plants you see below are all indigenous. Most of the trees in the mountains, such as aspens, pines, oaks, and willows have been here for thousands of years. American Indians, pioneers, and more modern people also brought seeds and plants from other places. Our most important farm crops are not indigenous to Utah. Seeds for corn, tomatoes, onions, and wheat were brought here. Peach, apple, apricot, and cherry trees were all brought here, too.

American Indians used plants for food and medicine. So did other early settlers. Pioneers made dandelion roots into medicine. They used dried cattails to stuff mattresses. They made dry weeds into brooms. They used juice from roots and berries to dye cloth in different colors. They used milkweed for chewing gum.

Sego Lilies

Our state flower is the sego lily. The early pioneers dug the bulbs and ate them not because they liked them, but because they were starving. They were described as "almost tasteless, but all right when cooked." Some sego bulbs were as large as hens' eggs, but most were about the size of marbles.

"I watched Indian women go out every day and return loaded with . . . sego and thistle roots to store for the winter," said a pioneer man.

Aroet Hale told of eating the bulbs to "show to our children and the rising generation how their parents suffered in the early days."

Cattails   Sagebrush

Pine

Joshua

Juniper

Cottonwood

Aspen

Today Utah has only two herds
of buffalo. One herd is on Antelope
Island in the Great Salt Lake.
The other is in the Henry Mountains.
There used to be many more
buffalo here.

It is up to everyone to help conserve natural resources and protect the environment. Even children can help. They can stop littering. They can recycle cans and paper. They can turn off lights and televisions when they aren't using them. Everyone can help prevent wildfires caused by humans. Everyone can be careful to take care of Utah.

1983 was a very wet year.
There were mud slides and floods
all over the state. This Bountiful
neighborhood was near a
mountain. Mud slid down and
covered roads and yards. It went
into the basements of people's
homes. They had to work together
to clean up the damage.

Our Changing Land

Utah's land is always changing. Some change is very slow. You already know how erosion slowly wears away rock and soil. Natural events such as mud slides happen fast. Sometimes when there is a lot of melting snow or rain, mountain clay gets so wet it breaks loose and slides down into the valley below. If there is a stream in the valley, the mud acts as a dam and water floods out over the land. Rock slides, avalanches, and earthquakes also change Utah land quickly. Our state has over seven hundred earthquakes each year, but most of them are too small to even feel.

People also change Utah's land. They build cities and freeways. They dig irrigation ditches to bring water to crops and orchards. In the mountains they make roads, cut trees, and build campgrounds. They plant new trees. They build huge dams that make reservoirs and new lakes. They dig into the ground to get the coal, oil, and copper. These things can be important for people. They provide homes, food, fuel, and jobs.

If people and industries are not careful, though, they can harm the environment. Many years ago, people often did not take care of the land very well. They thought people could never use up all the grass, trees, animals, and other resources. They thought there would always be plenty of fresh air and clean water.

Then, about the time Utah became a state, people began to think about using natural resources wisely. They passed laws to make it illegal for people or factories to pollute the air and water. They set aside some land for state and national parks, national forests, and wildlife refuges. Later, wilderness regions were set aside. There can be no roads or buildings there. People have to hike in or ride horses. They must be careful to leave no trace that they have been there. Today, most people are working together to keep our state a good place to live.

What Do You Think?

1. From what you know about the geography of Utah, do you think Utah would be hard or easy to settle? Why?

2. In what ways do people have to adapt to the land they live on?

3. Is life in Utah easier in the mountains, the plateaus, or the basins and valleys?

4. Should Utah advertise our beautiful scenery more so people from around the world will visit here? What would be the best and worst things that could happen?

5. What would happen if everyone who visited a state or a national park took home a plant or a rock?

6. What would happen if we all left our garbage wherever we wanted?

Can You Remember?

1. Describe where Utah is located in the world.

2. What are Utah's three main landforms?

3. What are some of Utah's important minerals?

4. What ancient lake used to cover a lot of Utah?

5. Name some of Utah's national parks.

6. Name some of Utah's wild animals.

Geography Tie-In

1. What continent is Utah on? Which oceans touch our continent?

2. Draw a picture of life on the land region where you live. Draw some of the animals and plants that live there. Draw some of the people who live there.

Words to Know

basin	indigenous
continent	paleontologist
erosion	petrified
extinct	plateau
fossil	sediment
geography	sedimentary rock
glacier	

Anasazi people used this sturdy wooden ladder to climb up out of pit houses and kivas. They were used to climb to the top rooms in cliff dwellings.

Early People Lived Here

History is the story of what has happened in the past. Utah history is the story of many, many different kinds of people. It tells what happened while they were here. People began coming to Utah a long time ago. First one group came, then another, and another. Today just about every kind of person you can think of lives in Utah.

There are people of all ages. In a house on your street may live a man with white hair who is 80 years old, or even older. There may be a new baby girl in the house next door. There are people from almost every country you can imagine. People have come here from Mexico and England and Africa and Vietnam and Russia and many other places. They are married and not married. They live in families, and they live alone. They belong to many religions. They may belong to no religious group.

Who were the first people to come here? They lived not just in our region, but all over North and Central and South America. An explorer named Christopher Columbus first called them Indians. When he landed in the Americas in 1492, he thought he was in a part of the world called East India. So he called the people he met "Indians." Now we usually call these people American Indians, or Native Americans, because they were "native" to America. They were here first. Both terms are all right to use. In their languages, they usually called themselves a name that meant "the people."

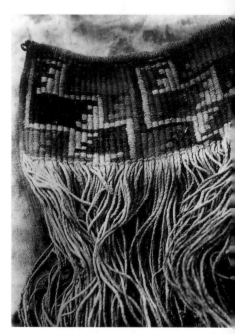

This Anasazi loin gown is made of thistle fiber, yucca fiber, and human hair.

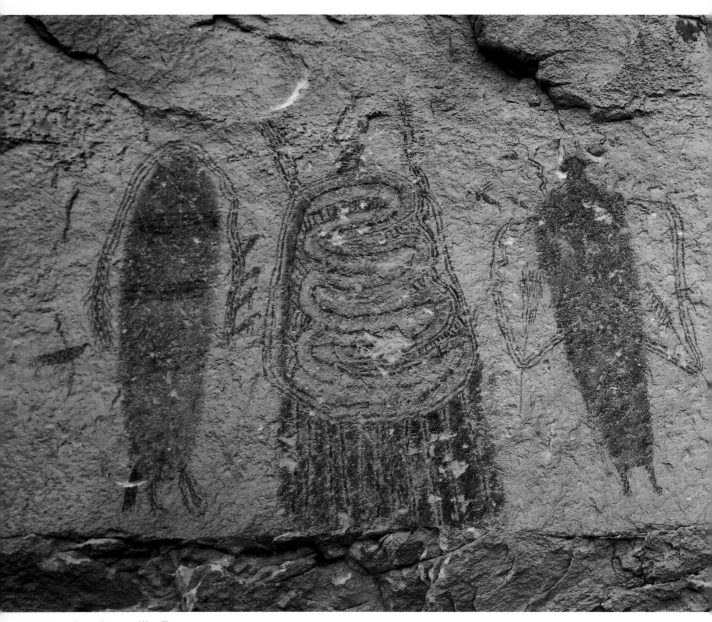

These human-like figures were made by combining art of birds, animals, and plants. The tallest image is about four feet tall. This rock art is found in the Moab region.
(Photo by Craig Law)

We don't have newspapers or books or letters written by the people who lived here so long ago. We don't have any diaries from them. We think they did not have a written language. How do you think we can find out about them?

We can find out about Native Americans long ago from the things they left behind. We can also learn some things from their drawings and paintings. They told stories about themselves, too. Stories have been handed down through families. It is like how grandmothers and grandfathers tell stories now about when they were young. Native Americans today continue to tell about themselves in their art and

"Many of our people went to the rock writing for medicine. If somebody had been sick a long time and wanted to be healed, people took him to the rock writings and left him there. This person would ask for the spirit to come and heal him. A lot of times they would get that blessing and be healed."

—*Mae Timbiboo Parry,*
Northwest Shoshone
(Oral History Institute)

stories. It is important to know what Native Americans say about their history.

Paleo-Indians

The earliest people we know of who lived here were the Paleo-Indians. Paleo means ancient, or very old. We do not know for sure, but they probably were here at least 12,000 years ago. One historian said, "They came so long ago that no one remembers the details."

This was not the only place Paleo-Indians lived. They lived all over the Americas, all over what we now call the

"So I was taught that these are our legal documents, our books. They explain who we are as a people, who we are as clans.... when people destroy rock art, they are destroying our ... documented history."

—*Wilfred Numkena, Hopi*
(Oral History Institute)

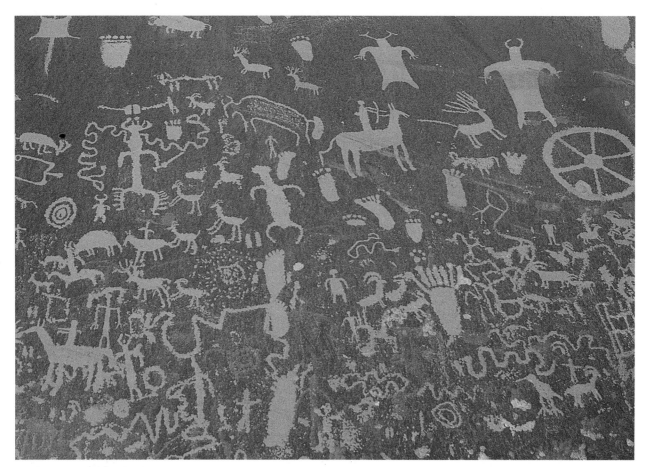

Newspaper Rock shows many animals, people, and symbols that American Indians painted and carved. It is in the Canyonlands region.

"To us what is known as rock art is not art. It is a documentation of spiritual events that happened at various sites. ... If you visit these sites, the thing you need to do is come with spiritual respect, because they are sacred sites. You had many spiritual events and ceremonies take place there."

—Wilfred Numkena, Hopi (Oral History Institute)

United States, Canada, Mexico, and Central and South America. They lived from the coldest parts of Canada to the tip of South America.

How did the people get here? Many scientists think they came from another part of the world called Asia. They traveled by foot. They walked over what was dry land. That dry land is now under the ocean. It is the bottom of what is called the Bering Sea between Siberia and Alaska. That is what scientists think. Some groups of people may have come here on boats.

Some Native Americans today believe that their people have always been here. One man said, "I was not brought from a foreign country and did not come here. I was put here by the Creator." Other Native Americans believe that there are many worlds. The one we live in is one of them. They believe that long ago their ancestors came from another world to this one. They emerged from a dark, underground world. The Dineh, or Navajo, believe that the First People followed Coyote and Badger from the center of the Earth to the outside.

Nomadic Hunters

One thing we know about Paleo-Indians is that they were **nomadic** hunters. They did not stay in one place for very long. Instead they followed animals wherever they went and killed them for food. Many of the animals they hunted do not exist any more, like the saber-toothed tiger, an early type of camel, and the woolly mammoth. Mammoths were very large animals. They were relatives of elephants and were the size of elephants. Can you imagine how hard it would be to kill such a large animal? How would you do it?

We also know about the spear points Paleo Indians made to hunt with. They made scrapers out of stone. They used the scrapers and chipped away the edges of a hard stone to make the points. The hunters lashed the points to strong thin sticks. Everything they used to make the spears was found in nature.

Besides hunting animals for food, these people must have gathered seeds, nuts, and other wild plants to eat. They probably did not grow gardens. No one knows for sure.

Desert Gatherers

After the Paleo people another group lived here. We call them Archaic Indians, or Desert Gatherers. Like the Paleo people, Desert Gatherers also lived all over North America and not just here. They were here for a long time. They lived here from about 8,000 years ago to about 1,600 years ago. That is much longer than any other group of people have ever lived here.

Desert Gatherers lived in small nomadic family groups. They moved from place to place all during the year. They were hunter-gatherers. They knew what could be found in certain places at certain times. In the spring the families lived around lakes and marshes. They collected duck eggs and new, tender cattail plants. They fished for trout. In the summer they moved to the mountains and hunted deer and gathered berries. In the autumn they gathered nuts and seeds and prepared for winter.

The people knew a lot about using the land to live. They knew all about animals—where they lived and how they acted. They knew where they could find fresh water to drink. They knew where to find stone for making spear points and tools. If a child was alone, she knew how to stay alive. She knew how to find water and food. She knew how to make a fire and how to catch fish. Could you do that?

To hunt, the Desert Gatherers used a weapon they invented called the **atlatl** (at'l at'l). It was a spear thrower. It was used before people invented the bow and arrow. A dart with a stone point on one end was laid in the atlatl. Then it was held over the shoulder. The hunter launched the dart by holding onto the atlatl and thrusting it forward. This shot the dart farther and harder than it could be thrown without the atlatl.

Plants Helped the People

The people could not have lived without plants. They learned how to use the roots, stems, flowers, and leaves. Here are three common plants the people used in many ways:

Rabbit Brush
■ Stems were used for making arrows.
■ Leaves were used to treat colds, fevers, and pain.
■ Flowers were boiled to make light yellow dye.
■ Stems were burned as fuel to keep kivas warm.

Using Plants

The Desert Gatherers had to be very skilled people. They could not just go to the store and buy what they needed. They had to know about hundreds of plants. They ate the bulbs of the sego lily and the roots of more than one hundred other plants. They gathered berries of all kinds. They knew which ones were poisonous and which ones were good to eat. They gathered acorns and grass seeds and sunflower seeds.

Pine nuts were also a very important food. Pine nuts are delicious little nuts inside the cones of certain kinds of pine trees. Desert Gatherers stored hundreds of pounds of pine nuts to eat during the winter. They also used the nuts to make soup. Sometimes they used the shells to make tea. For gum, they chewed the sticky sap from the nuts. During years when not many nuts were found, people could die of starvation.

After the Desert Gatherers collected nutritious seeds and nuts, they put them on a slab of stone called a *metate*. They held another stone called a *mano* to grind them up. Soon the ground-up seeds were like flour. Then they put the flour into a grass basket. They added water to make mush, and they cooked the mush. But they could not put the basket on a campfire. It would burn up. So they put hot stones from their campfire into the basket. The heat from the stones cooked the mush.

Desert Gatherers of long ago knew how to make waterproof baskets out of grass. They knew how to make grass nets to catch fish. They used plants to make sandals. The people knew which plants to use for medicine.

Pine Nuts

Pine nuts are still important today. You can buy them in stores in the late summer. You can also go into the mountains and find them.

Anita Whitefeather Collins is a Paiute. Every autumn her family goes into the mountains. They use poles to knock down the pinecones from the branches of the trees. They toss the pinecones into a cone-shaped basket, or *wudup*, to carry on their backs. Sometimes they collect more than twenty pounds of nuts in one day. At night they gather around a fire and take the nuts out of the cones.

When they get home, they use the nuts to make soup. They use a process similar to that of the Desert Gatherers. First they use a grinding stone to crack the shells of the nuts. Then they boil the nuts until they are soft. Next they grind up the nuts into flour. They add water to make a thick, healthful soup. It tastes sweet, rich, and smoky.

Yucca

This prickly plant grows all over in dry desert regions.
■ Young flower stalks, flowers, and fruit were eaten raw or roasted.
■ Roots were crushed with stones and used for soap.
■ The strong leaf fibers were woven into strong sandals. They were twisted and braided into rope. Blankets, floor mats, and baskets were made from it.
■ Sharp tips of leaves were used for paintbrushes to decorate pottery.

Willow

■ The wood was used for roofs. The strong branches held up the heavy dirt that was put on top.
■ The straight stems were made into arrows.
■ The wood was chewed to relieve pain.

Hogup and Danger Caves

Most of what we know about the Desert Gatherers in Utah comes from two caves in the west desert near Wendover. They are called Hogup Cave and Danger Cave. Desert Gatherers lived in them part of the year. Later, other groups of Native Americans lived in them.

About sixty years ago **archaeologists** discovered the caves and found all kinds of artifacts left thousands of years ago. They had been covered up by sand and dirt. Archaeologists had to **excavate** them (dig them up very carefully). Here is what they found:

nets—probably used to trap rabbits

animal skins

rope

mats and rugs

sandals

stone tools

grinding stones

seeds

purses and bags

small twigs cut and bent into shapes like deer

shells from the Pacific Ocean by California (How do you think they got to Utah?)

David Madsen was the Utah state archaeologist. Here he is digging in Hogup Cave. He and other archaeologists found many artifacts of the Desert Gatherers. They found tools, weapons, animal figures, clothes, and many other things.

These tiny deer are small enough to hold in your hand. Someone long, long, ago made them of split twigs. You can see them at the Utah Museum of Natural History at the University of Utah.

Discovery Detectives

Imagine this. Suppose a volcano erupted near your town. (Volcanoes used to be in Utah.) People hurried away just in time. But everything in their houses was buried under tons of lava, rock, and dirt. Hundreds of years later, maybe thousands of years later, archaeologists came. They began to dig down and find the buried town, and your house.

Archaeologists are like detectives. They look for clues about how people used to live. Things they find are called artifacts. Artifacts are things people made and used, like tools, weapons, toys, and dishes. What kinds of artifacts would archaeologists find in your house? Perhaps dishes, furniture, games, clothes, food? From those artifacts, what could they tell about you and the people you live with? What could they tell about the kind of work you do?

The Fremont and the Anasazi

Desert Gatherers lived in Utah for a long time. They were here for thousands of years. We do not know why they left. But after they did, two new groups of people lived in Utah. We call one of the groups the Fremont people. We call the other group the Anasazi. *Anasazi* is a Navajo word that means "ancient ones."

The Fremont and the Anasazi were similar in some ways. They both hunted, and they both farmed. They grew corn, beans, and squash. They made beautiful pottery. They were not nomadic like the Paleo-Indians and the Desert Gatherers. They both built **permanent** houses of wood, stone, and earth. Their houses were snug and efficient and were heated by fire.

People of the same tribe lived together in villages. They had to think about what other people wanted to do. They had to decide what to do when people had arguments. They had to work together and learn to cooperate.

The Fremont People

The houses the Fremont built were called **pit houses**. They were built partly underground, so that the earth formed all or part of the walls. They took a lot of work to build. The people dug large holes in the ground, kind of like digging out a basement. Then they cut poles from straight trees to hold up the roof. Branches were laid across the top, then covered with earth. There was always a fire pit in the middle.

The largest Fremont village ever discovered is called Five-Finger Ridge. It is located south of Richfield. Not long ago, a highway was built. When the workers were moving earth to make the highway, they found many ruins and **artifacts**. A large group of Fremont people had lived there. It is now part of Fremont Indian State Park.

Fremont Artifacts

These artifacts left by the Fremont people show how they used what they found in nature to make what they needed.

Burden basket made from plant fibers.

Bowl and jar made from earth clay.

Mitten made from antelope hide.

Moccasins. The small one is from Promontary Cave, made of buffalo hide. The large one is deer hide and was found in Hogup Cave.

Fremont and Anasazi

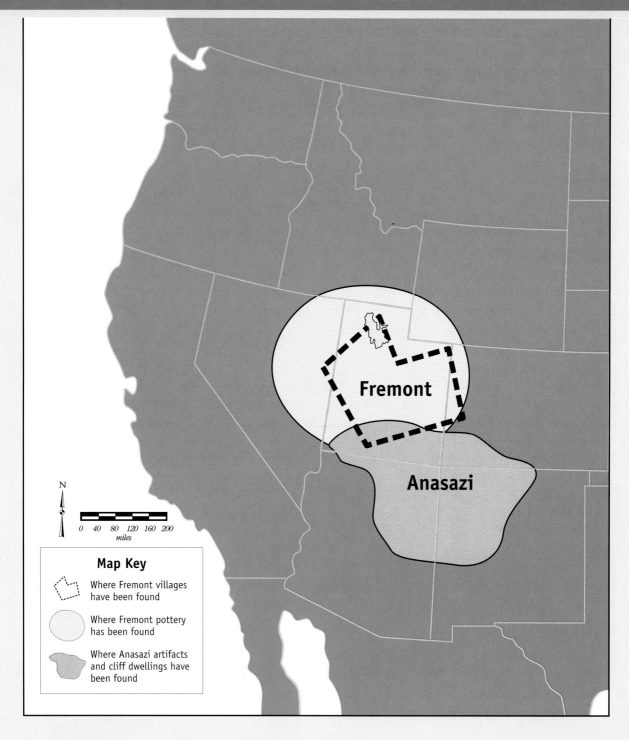

N

0 40 80 120 160 200
miles

Map Key

Where Fremont villages
have been found

Where Fremont pottery
has been found

Where Anasazi artifacts
and cliff dwellings have
been found

Fremont

Anasazi

The Fremont people made small figures out of clay that looked like people. They decorated them with necklaces and painted their faces. Archaeologists are not sure what the Fremont did with them. Maybe they used the figures in religious ceremonies. Perhaps they were toys for children. Maybe the people liked to make things, just like we do today.

The Fremont people hunted a lot. They hunted deer, mountain sheep, bison, antelope, rabbits, and whatever else they could find. They used the bow and arrow. With it they could shoot farther and harder than they could with the atlatl. They also gathered plants, seeds, and berries.

The Anasazi People

The Anasazi lived at the same time as the Fremont people, but in another region. They lived along the canyons and mesas of the San Juan River. This is where present-day Utah, Colorado, New Mexico, Arizona come together. It is called the four corners area. Can you tell why? Many more people lived there at that time than live in that area today.

Hidden away on the side of a cliff, this home is now deserted.
The strong walls were made of stones and mud.

The Anasazi were farmers. They grew cotton and wove it into belts and shirts. They grew food crops such as corn and beans and squash for the large groups of people who lived together. They all worked to grow the food. Then they carried it in baskets, dried it, and stored it for winter. In the ruins of Anasazi cliff dwellings whole rooms have been found that were used to store food.

Photo by Tom Till ▶

The region the Anasazi lived in was very dry. There was not enough rainfall to grow crops. They built small dams and lakes, called reservoirs, to catch rain when it did fall. Then they saved it to water their crops.

The people hunted with bows and arrows. Deer and rabbits had better watch out! The people were good hunters.

Anasazi children lived with their families in a beautiful place, with high plateaus and canyons. They kept dogs as pets, and raised turkeys to eat.

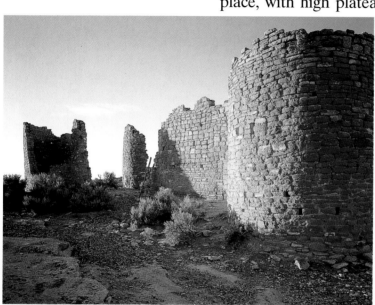

At first the Anasazi built very small farming villages. Not very many people lived in them. Later they built larger villages with cliff houses. These were like tall apartment buildings in the sides of cliffs. They were built with mud and stone and wood. Heavy, strong tree branches were cut and hauled to the place where the building was going to be. The branches were placed across the tops of the stone or adobe walls. Then another layer could be built on top of the first. The walls were painted with beautiful designs in red, yellow, black, and white colors. The Anasazi made the paint themselves. They used dye from plants and minerals.

One of the largest Anasazi villages is called Hovenweep. Today, you can see what is left of it. It is partly in Utah and partly in Colorado.

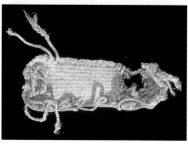

Anasazi sandals made of yucca fibers.

Sometimes these cliff houses were five stories high with hundreds of rooms. The Anasazi also built big houses on the top of flat hills. They were the first people in our region to build apartments to live in. The houses were hard to build and took a lot of work.

Both the Fremont and the Anasazi people are known for their rock art. Everywhere they lived they painted and carved pictures on canyon walls. They drew animals and people and symbols that meant something to them. Sometimes they seem to tell stories. Early people from all over the world did the same thing.

The Anasazi made baskets, and beautiful orange pottery with red and black painted designs. They made bags out of small animal skins. They padded cradle boards for carrying babies. They made necklaces, and carved whistles out of bone. They made stone knives with wooden handles.

Photo by John George ◄

Utah Museum of Natural History, University of Utah ◄

The Anasazi also built underground rooms called **kivas**. People gathered in them to talk and have religious ceremonies. Sometimes they painted sacred animals and spirits on the walls of the kivas.

A kiva was an underground meeting place for the men. They used it for religious ceremonies.

(Photo by John George)

Long Ago

Long Ago, the Mokweetch [Ute name for ancient Hopi ancestors] lived high along the cliff sides. My grandfather told me, there was a large eagle that would prey upon them. Therefore, to shelter themselves from these birds, they made their houses in the cliffs. The land looked the same as now, and the Mokweetch gathered plants and carried them in big baskets made of deer hide. They gathered the fruit of the yucca, choke cherries, wild onions, pinenuts, and all the other berries around.... they placed the food in their baskets and stored it there.

They also used the deer. They dried its meat, stored it, and made clothing from its hide. They would stretch the hide on top of a rock and remove the animal's hair. To cure the hide, they used the brain of the animal, rubbed it on. This made the hide smooth, then they smoked it.

During the winter, they wore thicker skins or several layers of buckskin with the hair left on. When it was hot during the summer, they just wore a breech cloth.

Their shoes were also made of hides and the fiber of the yucca and the cedar. Using needles of oak or bone, they sewed the leather onto the fiber.

But the people lived in constant fear. They were constantly on the move, looking out for these large birds, much larger than today's eagle, that bothered them. They feared these birds because they swooped down and took the people and fed them to their babies. So they never had permanent homes. Unlike the white man, they always moved from place to place. They came from these people, my grandfather said.

—*Lola Mike*
White Mesa Ute
Translated by Aldean Ketchum

What Do You Think?

Talk with other people about these things:

1. Archaeologists have learned a lot about early people. What are some of the facts? What things might be opinion?

2. If you were to suddenly move and leave everything you own right where it is now, what could someone in a thousand years learn about you from your things? What could they not know?

3. From what you read about how they lived, compare the lives of the Fremont and Anasazi with the Desert Gatherers. Which group would you rather be a part of?

Can You Remember?

1. How long ago do scientists think Native Americans lived in Utah?

2. What kind of evidence has been found that the people lived here?

3. What did the people do to survive?

4. Describe the Desert Gatherer way of life.

5. What can we learn today from people who lived here thousands of years ago?

Geography Tie-In

1. Study the map on page 32. It shows the large land regions where the people lived. Which groups lived nearest where you live?

2. Movement is one of the themes of geography. What or who moved from place to place in this chapter? Why did they move so much?

Words to Know

archaeologist

artifact

atlatl

excavate

kiva

nomad

permanent

pit house

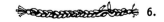

**These drawings show how to make rope
from the milkweed plant.**

This young Shoshone woman carries her baby on a cradle board.

3

American Indians Loved the Land

For thousands of years, different groups of American Indians were the only people living here. They were the first Utahns. Then, about 250 years ago, other people started coming. The first to come were Spanish explorers and Catholic priests. Later fur trappers came, and then the Mormon pioneers. They all wrote in their diaries and letters about the American Indian people they met.

Five main groups of American Indians were living here when the others arrived. They lived in different regions of what we now call Utah. They were the Goshutes, the Paiutes, the Utes, the Shoshones, and the Navajos. Those are the names others gave them. That is not what they called themselves. They called themselves names that in their language meant "the people." The Goshutes' name for themselves was *Kusiutta*. The Shoshone were *Nimi*. Paiutes called themselves *Nuwuvi*. Utes were *Nuciu*. Navajo were *Dineh*.

A Goshute woman and her child pose for a photograph in the late 1800s.

Food for Their Families

The Navajo were mainly farmers and ranchers who settled in one place. They also hunted a little. They lived in dry areas with very little rain. It was a lot of hard work, but they built irrigation ditches to bring water to their crops. They raised sheep and goats they got from the Spanish, and built wooden corrals.

The Utes gathered seeds and berries to make a kind of granola bar. They mixed the seeds and berries with animal fat and dried meat.

The Goshutes found uses for more than one hundred different kinds of plants. They also ate insects and crickets, which they ground up and made into cakes.

Photo by Jerry Jacka ◄

Today Sarah Whitehorse, a Navajo, raises sheep like her great-great-grandmother did over a hundred years ago. Notice the fence made of tree branches.

The Navajo people generally lived in one area most of their lives. Utes, Paiutes, Goshutes, and Shoshones, however, lived a nomadic way of life. They did not settle in one place and raise their own food as the Navajos did. Instead they traveled around, searching for plants and animals to eat. Often the families lived near the beautiful lakes and rivers. Fish and ducks and other water birds became a tasty dinner.

Some groups of Paiutes in Southern Utah farmed. They planted corn, squash, beans, sunflowers, wheat, and melons. The Shoshones and the Goshutes also planted seeds from some wild plants. However, they were not full-time farmers.

The people probably talked and laughed together as they made bowls and baskets out of plant leaves and stems. They needed the baskets to carry the seeds, nuts, and roots in. They also made water jugs.

How did they eat the nuts and seeds they found? They could eat them out of their hand, of course. The people also ground up seeds and nuts into flour, like their ancestors had done for hundreds of years, and like we do today. With the flour, they made cakes and baked them.

Historic American Indians in Utah

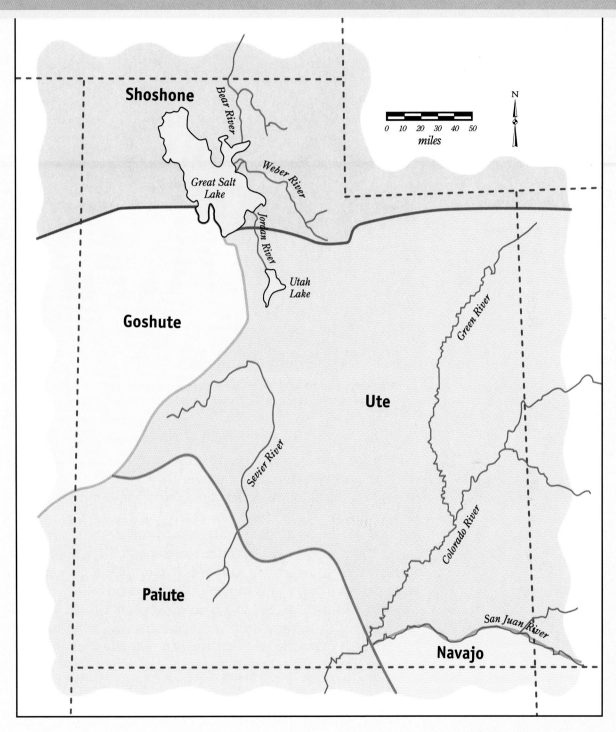

Shoshone

Bear River

Weber River

Great Salt Lake

Jordan River

Utah Lake

Goshute

Ute

Green River

Sevier River

Colorado River

Paiute

San Juan River

Navajo

N

0 10 20 30 40 50
miles

Buffalo meat jerky was made by drying strips of meat on wooden racks in the sun. It lasted a long time without going rotten.

A horse pulls a travois. Travois were often used by Utes and Shoshones for carrying heavy loads. Children often got to ride on them!

Hunting Wild Animals

With bows and arrows, spears, clubs, and knives American Indians hunted whatever animals they could find. There were deer, buffalo, elk, mountain sheep, antelope, rabbits, and squirrels. The Paiutes hunted mainly in groups. They figured out a way to get squirrels and other small animals out of their holes in the ground. Someone made a hook and stuck it into the animal's burrow. The hook caught on the animal's fur. Then it was pulled out of its burrow.

For a long time the men, women, and children traveled everywhere on foot. Later, some groups got horses from the Spanish explorers. At first they used the horses as pack animals. Later they started to ride them. Then they could travel over larger areas. The Goshutes and Paiutes did not use horses to help them hunt. The Utes, Shoshones, and Navajos all used horses for hunting, moving about, and to carry heavy loads.

Buffalo were very important to the Shoshones and the Utes. They ate its meat, and they used every part of it for something. They used its fur for winter blankets. They used its skin to make tepees and clothing.

Clothes from Plants and Animals

Not all the people dressed alike. Some of them wore animal skins, sometimes with the fur still on. They also wove different grasses and bark to make clothes. Some used animal hides to cover their feet. They also wove reeds and plants into strong sandals. The Navajo people raised sheep, and used the wool to make yarn. They dyed the yarn with colors from different plants. Then they wove beautiful rugs, blankets, and cloth.

Ute men wore shirts and leggings made out of buffalo skins. Ute women also wore leggings and long dresses or skirts. They all wore moccasins. At special times, like during the Sun Dance and the Bear Dance, Ute men wore fancy feathered headdresses. They painted their bodies and faces with black and yellow designs. The men did not cut their hair. They wore long braids.

The Goshutes lived on the hot desert land. In summer they did not need to wear many clothes. Goshute men wore a breechcloth. Goshute women wore aprons or grass skirts. Sometimes they wore sun shades made of twigs on their heads. In winter the families had rabbit skin blankets to help them keep warm. They usually did not wear moccasins.

The Paiute people also wore few clothes. In summer children wore nothing. Men wore breechcloths, and women wore skirts. In winter everyone wore shirts and used blankets made from soft rabbit skins.

After the explorers and settlers came, they opened trading posts and sold cotton shirts, pants, and dresses to the American Indians. In most of the photographs in this book the American Indian people are wearing a mixture of traditional clothes and more modern clothes, shoes, and hats.

These Paiute children are wearing leather clothes. The weather must have been cool when the picture was taken.

A Ute child, dressed in leather, helps care for her baby brother or sister. Notice the corn hanging to dry.

Making a Home

American Indians did not all live in the same kinds of houses. Navajos built different houses than Utes and Shoshones did. A Navajo family built a **hogan** to live in. It was meant to be filled with happiness. While it was being built, people sang songs. The hogan stood for the Navajo's spiritual connection to Mother Earth. Its door always faced east, to meet the rising sun. Family hogans were spaced far apart from each other. Navajos did not live in villages.

Paiutes and Goshutes lived in family groups, called clans, of fifteen to thirty people. They lived in small villages. They built as many houses as they needed close to each other. Their houses were called **wicki-ups**. They were made of branches and brush. Sometimes the builders covered them with animal skins. Goshutes lived in the wicki-ups only in the summer. In the winter they lived in caves and rock shelters to stay warmer.

Utes and Shoshones built **tepees** to live in. They were made of buffalo skins and tall poles. Tepees could be taken down and carried like tents. In the center of a tepee, the family built a fire on the ground. They cooked on the fire and used it to keep the tepee warm. The smoke went out a hole in the top of the tepee.

> "After the first hogan was built, everyone rested. The First Woman lay with her feet to the west, and the First Man lay with his feet to the east. Their heads crossed and their thoughts mingled, and these thoughts were sacred."
>
> —*Navajo Tradition*

Navajo hogans are made of logs and earth. They are cool in summer and, with a fire inside, can be warm in winter. Some Navajo people still live in hogans.

Like the Paiutes and Goshutes, the Ute and Shoshone people lived in villages. These were tribal groups of about two hundred people. The tribe was divided into smaller family clans. In a clan were fathers, mothers, and children. Grandparents and aunts, uncles, and cousins were part of the clan too.

Activity
Which Kind Would You Build?

Think about why each group built the kind of home, or shelter, they did. In a small group of friends, discuss these things:

1. Some tribes followed herds of animals and moved from place to place. Which shelter would be best for them? Why?

2. Some groups stayed in one place and farmed. Which house would be best for them?

3. What was each shelter made of? Why did the people use those materials? Why didn't they use brick, lumber, or glass?

4. What are the best things about the Indian homes?

5. What are some things about the homes that might have been a problem?

Paiute wicki-ups were summer homes, made of branches and brush.

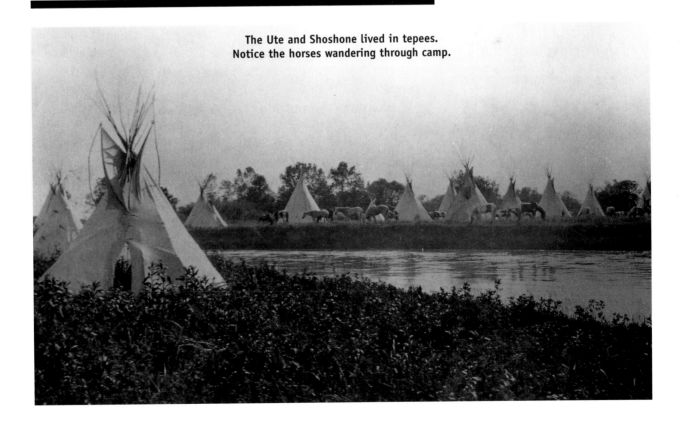

The Ute and Shoshone lived in tepees.
Notice the horses wandering through camp.

"There is a reverence
for everything.
Everything has a spirit.
There's a spiritual quality
about trees, about the
land, about the sun and
the moon."

—*Shirley Reed, Ute*
(Interview with Oral History
Institute, 1996)

"I want clear thinking,
clear understanding.
That's what I say when I
pray. I want to be right
for others. I care for
people. I love people."

—*Jensen Jack, White River*
Ute Elder, Sun Dance Chief,
and Medicine Man
(Interview with Oral History
Institute, 1996)

A Spiritual People

All of the different groups of American Indians were spiritual people. Sometimes a whole group came together to sing and pray. Sometimes just two or three people would. Sometimes an older person prayed for all of them. Some Indian groups believed in one god. God, and god's power, was present in all things, especially things in nature. Other Indian peoples believed in many gods, or many spirits. This is still true today.

One of the Navajo gods was Grandfather of the Gods. He was also called Talking God. Here is a Navajo poem about him:

I, I am Talking God. Now I Wander About.
From under the East I wander about. Now I wander about.
The Dawn lies toward me. I wander about. Now I wander about.
The white corn lies toward me. Now I wander about.
Before me it is beautiful. It shows my way.
Behind me it is beautiful. It shows my way.

An important part of life for Indian peoples was a respect for nature. American Indians lived close to nature. They knew all about the land. They felt that they knew its secrets, and every part of it was special to them. The ground under their feet was more than just grass, rock, and dirt. The sun in the sky was more than just a ball of fire. They wanted to see and feel and touch the earth every day or they did not feel right.

Sharing was important to most Indian people. They were very generous in sharing within their tribe when others were in need. Usually they said that all land that people farmed and hunted on, and all rivers and lakes they fished in, belonged to everyone in the group. They believed that God made the earth for the common good of people. Everything on it was given to all. Everyone was entitled to a share.

Larry Cesspooch is a Ute. He and historian Kathryn MacKay said, "Nuche [Utes] traveled with the seasons. They went to high mountains in the summer, living by hunting small and big game animals and birds, fishing and gathering a variety of berries, nuts, seeds, and plants.... Hunting, fishing, and gathering sites were not owned.... [they were] communal [shared] and granted to all."

Photo by Jerry Jacka ▼

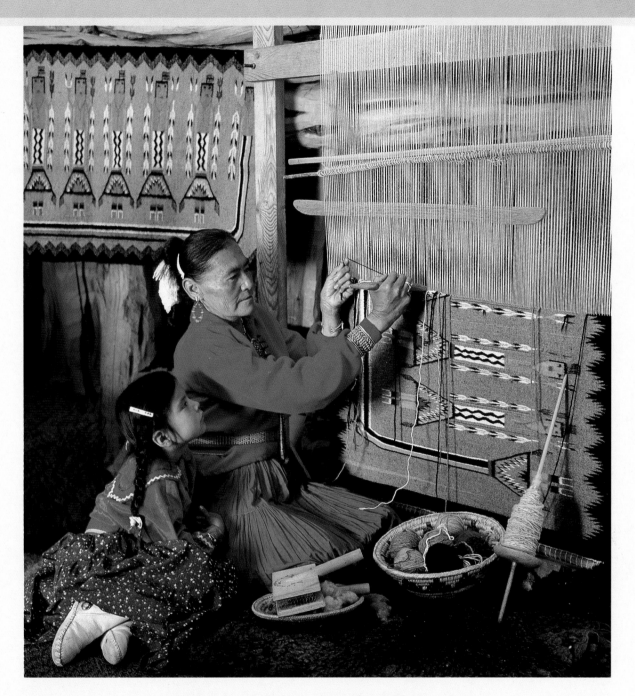

Harmony Between People and Nature

American Indians talked about **harmony** between people and nature. Navajos said, "We walk in beauty and harmony." Beauty was important to them. They wanted to follow a path of beauty through life. Today a Navajo woman named Suzie Yazzie shows her daughter how to make beautiful rugs. She says, "The whole philosophy of Navajo culture is one of beauty and harmony. That is what I am doing with my weaving. I am creating Navajo beauty from Navajo materials. Everything you see has come from Mother Earth, from the wool yarn to the dye from plants that grow around us—everything."

"I know I am
a good person, and so
are the things around me.
Trees are good, birds are good,
animals are good."

—*Shirley Reed, Ute social worker*
(Interview with Oral History Institute, 1996)

Animals and Birds

American Indians shared the land with animals and birds. They did not step on a snake's tracks in the sand or disturb a fox's den. They did not push a lizard out of the path. Trees, flowers, squirrels, and insects all had value. They said the land belongs to the spider and the ant and the deer the same as it does to people.

According to an old Navajo story, otter and beaver lent their skins to protect the Twin War Gods. Their father, the Sun, had tested the Twin War Gods by trying to freeze them. Bats were also special. They were messengers of the night. They gave protection. Dragonflies were messengers of the sun. Navajos said that the coyote brought fire to humans. Coyote stole it from the sleeping Fire God. The eagle gave people power and strength.

Horses were important to Utes and Shoshones. They valued and respected horses. When they wanted to get something, they made promises to the horse. If the horse would help them, they told it, they would paint it with beautiful designs and colors. Then everyone who saw it would know how helpful it had been.

The way to start a day
is this: Go outside and
face east, where the sun
is rising. When the first
pale streaks of light cut
through the darkness,
greet the sun with
a blessing or chant or
song. When you do this,
you help the sun come
up. When you do this,
you can also paint your
face, if you want to. Do
this because a morning
needs to be sung to.
A new day needs
to be honored.

Singing and Dancing

Songs and dances were important to American Indians. There was magic in singing and dancing. There was power in the music. They sang songs to protect hunters. They sang songs to make children grow strong and healthy. They sang songs to make corn grow. They danced, chanted, and played musical instruments to bring rain and make night winds blow.

Nicely, nicely, nicely, away in the east,
The rain clouds care
For the little corn plants
as a mother cares for her baby.
    —*Navajo Corn Ceremony*

Ute children perform the Bear Dance in 1920, just as they have for many years. The dance celebrates spring, when the bear comes out of its den after sleeping all winter.

Silence was also important to American Indians. Talking never started at once, nor in a hurried manner. No one was quick with a question. First there was a pause. This gave time for thought. This was the respectful, polite way of starting a talk with someone.

The moon will be created. They say he is planning it.
Its face will be white. They say he is planning it.
Its chin will be yellow. They say he is planning it.
Its horns will be white. They say he is planning it.
    —*Navajo Song of the Moon Creation*

Father, Mother, Sister, Brother

Families were important to American Indians. Today when Navajos meet new people, first they say their own names. Then they talk about their parents and grandparents. That way they remember who they are, where they came from, and where they belong. And everyone else knows too.

LeNora Begay is a Navajo girl who lives in Salt Lake City. When she meets a new person, this is what she says: "My name is LeNora Begay. My mother's clan is the Red Running into Water People. My father's clan is the Bitter Water People. The Tangle People and the Towering House People are my grandparents."

"We do not want riches. But we do want to train our children right. We want peace and love."

—*Ute saying*

The Hosteen Tsetso family were Navajos. They lived near the Utah-Arizona border. This picture was taken about fifty years ago.

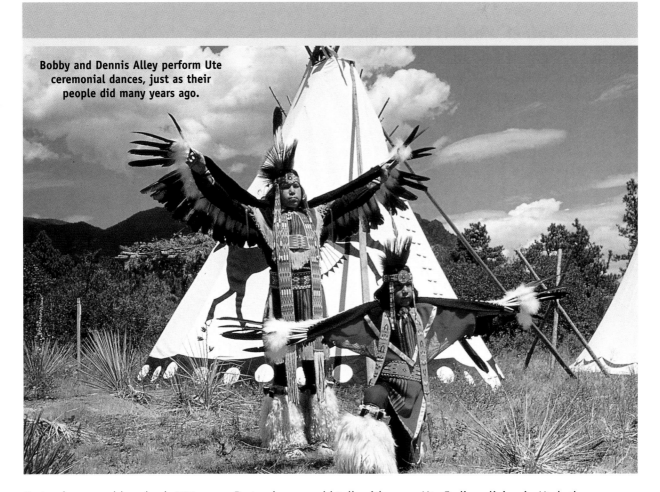

Bobby and Dennis Alley perform Ute ceremonial dances, just as their people did many years ago.

Photo by Jeannie Young ▲

Pretend you could go back 200 years. Pretend you could talk with some Ute Indians living in Utah then. You ask them to tell you about their people. They might say something like this:

We respect everything in life—the air, the wind, thunder and lightening. Rain, mountains, trees, flowers, animals, and water are all sacred to us.

Religion is important in our lives. We believe in a creator God. There is a god of war and a god of peace. There is a god who heals sick people and a god who rules the weather. We ask for blessings from the gods— to be healthy, to be brave, to be good hunters, and to be good parents to our children.

It is important to sing and dance. We have songs for everything. There are songs for good health and songs for good weather. There are songs for war and songs for peace.

Our families are important to us. Our families include fathers and mothers, brothers and sisters, uncles and aunts, grandparents and great-grandparents. We honor our old people. They are wise. We ask their advice. We serve them first at meals. We listen to their stories. We learn from them.

We admire good hunters. They also defend the people from danger. As boys grow up, they learn to hunt and fish. They learn to make rope, build fires, and clear ground for camps. They learn to make tools and weapons.

We admire strength in women, too. They take care of the family. When girls grow up, they learn to gather food and make baskets and pots. They make clothing and fix it when it gets torn. They haul wood and carry water.

We have many leaders, not just one. Both men and women are leaders. Both men and women belong to our tribal council.

Language and Legends

American Indian groups had spoken languages, but they did not write them down. When the trappers and pioneers met them, they had no alphabet. They could not write about their lives.

The people told stories instead. The old and wise people taught the young ones by telling them stories. The stories taught the history and honor of the clan or tribe. The stories also explained how things in nature happened. Such stories are called **legends**. Sometimes the stories were short. Sometimes they were very long. One Goshute story took more than six hours to tell!

You know that there are twelve months in a year, but do you know why? This Goshute legend explains.

Legends passed on the group's special **culture** to the young people. Culture means the way people lived and what they believed.

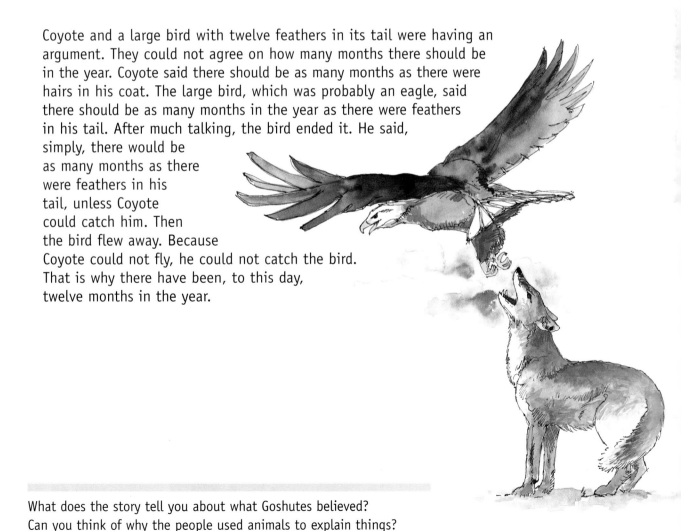

Coyote and a large bird with twelve feathers in its tail were having an argument. They could not agree on how many months there should be in the year. Coyote said there should be as many months as there were hairs in his coat. The large bird, which was probably an eagle, said there should be as many months in the year as there were feathers in his tail. After much talking, the bird ended it. He said, simply, there would be as many months as there were feathers in his tail, unless Coyote could catch him. Then the bird flew away. Because Coyote could not fly, he could not catch the bird. That is why there have been, to this day, twelve months in the year.

What does the story tell you about what Goshutes believed?
Can you think of why the people used animals to explain things?

Activity
Naming Utah Places

Did you know? Many places in Utah have American Indian names. Here are some of the names and what they mean. Some words are Paiute, some Ute, and some Goshute. Are any of these places near you?

Juab .... Flat or level (Ute)

Kamas .... Small grassy plain among hills (Ute)

Kanab .... Willow (Paiute)

Kanarraville .... Named for Paiute Chief Kanarra

Kanosh .... Man of white hair (Ute)

Koosharem .... Plant like a carrot with a root you can eat (Ute)

Oquirrh Mountains .... Wooded mountains (Goshute)

Panguitch .... Place where fish are (Paiute)

Paragonah .... Thin stream of salty water (Paiute)

Parowan .... Marsh people (Paiute)

Peoa .... Marry (Ute)

Santaquin .... Named for Ute Chief Santaquin

Tabby Mountains .... Named for Ute Chief Tabby

Timpanogos .... River in a rocky mountain (Ute)

Tintic .... Named for Ute Chief Tintic

Toquerville .... Black mountain (Paiute)

Uinta .... Pine land (Ute)

Wanship .... Named for Ute Chief Wanship

Wasatch .... Mountain pass (Ute)

Chief Tabby

What Do You Think?

Talk with other people about these things:

1. What was important to American Indians?

2. Are these same things important to you?

3. How did legends help the people?

4. How would your life be different if you did not have a written language?

5. What ideas from the American Indian culture could make your life better?

6. What things from your culture might have helped the American Indians?

Can You Remember?

1. What were the five main American Indian groups in our region when the Spanish priests, trappers, and pioneers came?

2. What were some of the main differences between the Navajos and the other groups?

3. What things from nature did the different groups use to make clothes?

4. What things from nature did the people use to make their homes?

5. How did American Indians get their food?

Geography Tie-In

1. Study the map on page 41 showing where the different groups lived. Compare it to the map on page 8 showing the land regions of Utah. Which groups lived near the mountains? The plateaus? The deserts?

2. Divide your class into teams. Look at a map of Utah in an atlas. See how many of the Utah places on page 54 your team can find.

Words to Know

culture

harmony

hogan

legend

tepee

wicki-up

A Navajo man shows a priest how to do a sand painting. Sand was colored with dried flowers, cornmeal, and plants. Sand paintings were used to make sick people feel better. People who were sick lay down on them, or the sand from them was sprinkled on their backs. The sand drew out the disease from the body. Then the sand was put in a place where the evil that had been absorbed by it could do no harm.
—*St. Christopher's Mission, Bluff*

Spanish explorers, wearing heavy clothes and carrying swords, explored the West. This is a painting of the explorers looking deep into the Grand Canyon of what is now Arizona. Maynard Dixon was the artist. He painted many western scenes.

4

Trappers and Explorers

T he first people to call the Utah region their home
were different groups of Native Americans. They
have been here for thousands of years. About
250 years ago, other people began coming here. In
this chapter we will discuss who they were, why they came,
and the adventures they had.

Explorers from Spain

The first non-Indians to come here were Europeans. They
came from a country in Europe named Spain. We call them
Spanish explorers. They explored the mountains and the
valleys. They made maps of Utah, and they wrote about it.

Columbus Explored the Americas

Spain was the country that sent Christopher Columbus to explore in 1492. Columbus did not intend to come to the Americas. He did not even know there was any land here. He was on his way to Asia. He landed here by mistake. He called this the New World. However, this was not really a new world. It had been here a very long time, and people had been living here for thousands of years.

While Columbus and his men were exploring the islands close to what is now Florida, they found many things they wanted. There was plenty of good land to grow crops. The crops would then be taken back to Spain and sold. There were gold and silver that could be mined. And the Spanish could force the Indians, as they called them, to work in the mines.

When Columbus went back to Spain, he forced some American Indians to go with him. He made them slaves, and he told everyone what he had found. Spain sent more people to the Americas. Soon Spain said much of the land belonged to them, and they began to **colonize** it. They built cities and towns. They started large farms, called plantations. They forced the Indian people to dig mines and to work in them. They sent large amounts of gold and silver back to Spain. The Spanish thought America and the people living there were theirs for the taking.

The Indian people had religions of their own, but the Spanish tried to make Indians live the Catholic religion.

Columbus and his crew landed far away from what is now Utah. But after his trips, many other Spanish people came. They came to Mexico and called it New Spain. Later, some of them came to our Utah region.

Christopher Columbus

Fathers Domínguez and Escalante

Soon the Spanish had many settlements in Mexico, Central America, and South America. They even had settlements in California and New Mexico. They wanted a route to get from Santa Fe, New Mexico, to Monterey, California. The trail would be used to send letters, supplies, and soldiers. In 1776 they sent twelve men to look for the best route. The two men in charge of the journey were Catholic priests, named Father Francisco Domínguez and Father Silvestre de Escalante.

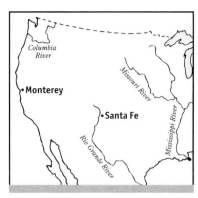

The explorers needed a way to get from Santa Fe to Monterey.

The Domínguez-Escalante **expedition** left Santa Fe for California with their pack animals and horses in hot July. They traveled northward all summer through dry country that was nothing like they had ever seen in Spain. Then they turned west into what is now Utah. They killed a buffalo

Catholic priests Father Escalante and Father Domínguez and their group enter the Utah Valley.
(Painting by P. Salisbury)

"We also saw that everywhere there were smoke signals . . . carrying in this way news of our arrival."

—*Father Escalante's journal, September 23, 1776*

Father Escalante wrote about the Ute people.

there and ate it. Ute Indians guided them and helped them find their way. One of the Indian guides was an eleven-year-old boy they named Joaquin. They would have had a hard time without his help.

After traveling for several weeks, they climbed up a ridge at the mouth of a canyon. Father Escalante wrote in his diary that they "caught sight of the lake and the spreading valley of *Nuestra Señora de la Merced de la Timpagonotzia.*" Today we call what they saw Mount Timpanogos, towering above Utah Valley, where Provo is now.

Father Escalante's Diary

For three days the group camped and talked with Utes near Utah Lake. This is part of what Father Escalante wrote in his **diary** about them:

> *They live on the lake's abundant fish. . . . Besides this, they gather the seeds of wild plants in the bottoms and make a gruel [mush] from them, which they supplement with the game of jackrabbits, and fowl, of which there is a great abundance. They also have bison handy not too far way. . . . They have interesting crafted baskets and other utensils for ordinary use.*

In his diary Father Escalante described every stream they crossed. He said the climate was warm. There was also plenty of firewood and timber in the mountains. The group did not see the Great Salt Lake, but the Utes told them about it. Here is what Father Escalante wrote about it in his diary:

> *Its waters are harmful and extremely salty, for the Timpanois assured us that anyone who wet some part of his body with them immediately felt a lot of itching in the part moistened.*

The Spaniards did not think they could find a way to cross the desert before winter began, so they turned back for Santa Fe. Although they did not find their way to California, Domínguez and Escalante did explore parts of Utah and map it. The diary of Father Escalante is an important way we have of finding out about early Utah. These Spanish explorers were among the many different people who have come to Utah. After they left, Spanish traders kept coming here for a long time. As a result, many places in Utah have Spanish names.

Domínguez–Escalante Route, 1776

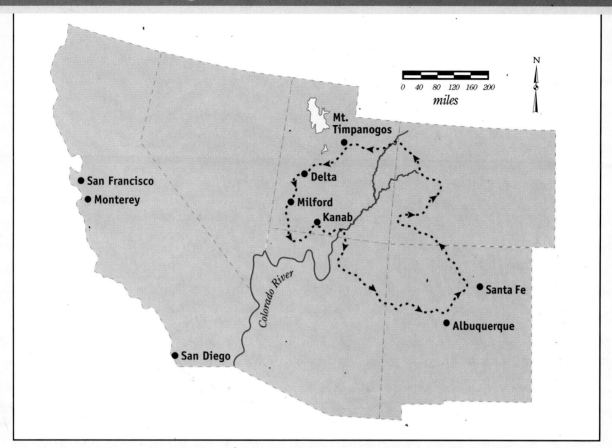

Activity
A New Trail

The Spanish wanted a trail to go from Santa Fe to Monterey. Twelve men went to look for the best route. They went up into what is now Utah, then returned to Santa Fe. They never got to Monterey.

1. On the map, find Santa Fe and Monterey. If the group had traveled straight to Monterey, how many miles would they have traveled?

2. Which major river would they have had to cross?

3. When the men left for their trip in 1776, there were no states in the West. In fact, the country of Spain claimed ownership of the land. Talk with your teacher about what was happening in our country on the East Coast during that time.

4. Look on a map of the United States today, and see which states the men would have had to travel through to get to Monterey. Which of today's states did they actually travel through?

Spanish Names in Utah

Abajo Mountains, San Juan County	**Abajo** means low
Arido Creek, San Juan County	**Arido** means dry
Boneta, Duchesne County	**Bonita** means graceful or beautiful
Castilla Springs, Utah County	First called **Aguas Calientes**, meaning hot waters
Dolores River, Grand County	First named **Rio Nuestra Señora de los Dolores**, meaning River of Our Lady of Sorrows; shortened to **Rio Dolores** or Dolores River
The Crossing of the Fathers	Place on the Colorado River, where Fathers Domínguez and Escalante crossed; first named **El Vado de los Padres**
Escalante Desert, Escalante River, Escalante (Town)	Named in honor of Father Escalante
Green River	Father Escalante named it **Rio Buenaventura**, meaning River of Good Fortune; later named **Rio Verde**, or Green River
La Sal Mountains	From **Sierra de Sal**, a mountain range of salt
Meadows of Santa Clara, Washington County	From **Las Vegas de Santa Clara** or Mountain Meadows, in **Santa Clara**
Virgin River, in Washington and Kane Counties	From **Rio de la Virgen**
San Rafael River	**Rio San Rafael**, named for San Rafael Archangel, the angel of the spirits of men
Salina (Town), Salina Creek, Salina Canyon, Sevier County	Named for the nearby rock salt; **salina** means a salt pond
San Juan River	From **Rio San Juan Bautista**, St. John the Baptist River
Sevier River	From **Rio Severo** in Sevier County
White River, Uintah County	From the Spanish **Rio Blanco**

Searching for Beaver

After the Domínguez-Escalante expedition, the next group of people to come to Utah were mountain men. They were fur trappers who searched the mountains and rivers of the West for beavers and other animals.

Beavers live near water, where there are many trees. They use trees to make their houses in lakes and streams. Their houses are partly underwater.

In those days a felt hat made from beaver fur was the best hat a person could buy. It was very popular with rich people. Everyone wanted one.

Altogether about 3,000 men, along with some women and children, came west to trap beavers and sell their skins. Mountain men were businessmen. They wanted to make a profit by selling beaver skins.

Mountain men found the streams of northern Utah loaded with beavers. In the 1820s and 1830s Utah became a center for the fur trade. Large fur companies hired trappers. The three main companies were from England, Mexico, and the United States.

High Fashion

The beaver hat was the reason the West was explored so much by the trappers. For over 100 years, no proper European gentleman was seen in public without one. The hat makers could hardly keep up with all the hats people wanted. Americans in the cities liked the hats, too, and paid a lot of money for them.

The trouble was, the trappers of Europe had killed all the beaver there. They needed American beaver fur for their hats.

People wanted fur for other reasons, too. It became popular for both ladies and gentlemen to wear fox, otter, and other animal fur on coat collars, sleeves, gloves, and boots.

Trappers Meet American Indians

American Indians had also trapped beaver and other animals for a long time. They sometimes guided mountain men to the best trails and beaver streams. Mountain men also got beavers from them. Many mountain men married Indian women. The men and their wives worked together to trap the beaver and to prepare the pelts for market. Some trappers spent winters in Indian villages.

Often, however, there were bad feelings between mountain men and Indian people. Mountain men came onto Indian lands without asking permission. They disturbed the people and their way of life. They prepared the way for permanent white settlement and the removal of Indians from their land. Indian peoples did not like this. To drive the trappers off their land, they often attacked the trappers and took their horses and furs. They wanted the trappers to leave and return to their own land.

After they came west mountain men often married American Indian women.

Famous Explorers

Some of the best known mountain men were Peter Skene Ogden, Jim Bridger, James Beckwourth, and Jedediah Smith.

Peter Skene Ogden explored the western deserts of Utah and Nevada. He led many trappers into the Great Basin. He kept a daily journal. It is one of the earliest written accounts of Northern Utah. It also helps us learn about the life of a mountain man.

In his diary Ogden wrote about when he first came into Utah. The land was swarming with huge black crickets and the air was filled with seagulls.

When he first entered Ogden Valley he called it a "hole," because mountains completely surrounded it. The city of Ogden and the Ogden River are named after him.

Jim Bridger was about twenty years old when he came to Utah to trap. He hadn't gone to school much in his life, but he was a great storyteller. He had been a blacksmith before becoming a fur trapper. The group he was trapping with entered what we now call Cache Valley. They camped on the Bear River. His men tried to guess where it ended. Bridger followed the river in a boat until it flowed into a large body of water. He tasted the water and discovered it was very salty. He thought he might have reached the Pacific Ocean. His men explored the lake for miles. Later he found out it was a great salty lake, and not the ocean at all. Without good maps, the explorers had to do a lot of guessing about where they were.

After his trapping days were over, Jim Bridger stayed in the West. He had an idea for a fort where travelers going farther west could stop.

Jim Bridger

A traveler on his way to California wrote the following about the Fort Bridger trading post: "They have a good supply of robes, deer, elk, and antelope skins, coats, pants, moccasins, flour, pork, powder, lead, blankets, butcher knives, spirits, ready-made clothes, coffee, and sugar."

Fort Bridger was built as a stopping place for travelers. It was also used by government soldiers. You can visit it today near Evanston, Wyoming.

James Beckwourth

Louis Vasquez, from New Mexico, and three other trappers paddled around the Great Salt Lake. They used boats made of animal skins. They looked for rivers flowing out of the lake. They also wanted to find the streams that flowed into the lake so they could trap beaver. They found the land around the lake to be very dry, with few trees. There were no rivers leaving the lake. And the lake was very salty.

After he stopped trapping, Vasquez became a businessman. He joined his friend Jim Bridger to help build the trading post at Fort Bridger. Later he ran stores in Colorado and Salt Lake City, and sold supplies the people needed.

James Beckwourth was one of the most famous mountain men. He wrote a book about his life. He was also an explorer, miner, army scout, and businessman. Beckwourth was born a slave in Virginia to a white father and a black mother. When James was a teenager, his father moved him to Missouri, where he did not have to be a slave. Soon afterward, James went west to be a trapper. A tribe of Crow Indians adopted him. He lived with them for several years and married a Crow wife. For the rest of his life, he often dressed like the Crows.

Beckwourth discovered a pass in the high Sierra Mountains between California and Nevada. People traveling to California in later years used this route.

Jedediah Smith took a Bible with him when he went west to trap. Sometimes he read to himself, and sometimes he read to other trappers around the evening campfire.

Jed walked and rode horses around many places in the West. Everywhere he went he had adventures. Not all of them were good! In South Dakota a grizzly bear attacked Jed. It ripped one of his ears and part of his scalp almost all the way off. Jed asked one of his friends, James Clyman, to sew his ear on again. Here is what Clyman wrote in his diary:

> One of his ears was torn from his head out to the outer rim after stitching all the other wounds in the best way I was capabl and according to the captains directions the ear being the last I told him I could do nothing for his Eare O you must try to stich up some way or other said he then I put in my needle stiching it through . . . as nice as I could.

On one of his many trips in search of beaver, Jedediah Smith left the Great Salt Lake region and traveled with other men through southwest Utah and through the dry land of Nevada and California. He was only twenty-seven years old. He and some companions trudged across the flat Mojave Desert in the burning autumn sun. They almost died because they couldn't find enough food or water.

They stayed through the winter, trapping beaver and other animals. Later, they crossed the high Sierra Nevada Mountains, crossed Nevada, and returned to Utah.

This is what Jedediah wrote in his journal about returning to Utah:

> *. . . The Salt Lake a joyful sight was spread before us. Is it possible said the companions of my sufferings that we are so near the end of our troubles. For myself I durst scarcely believe that it was really the Big Salt Lake that I saw. It was indeed a most cheering view. . . . But so it was with me for I had traveled so much in the vicinity of the Salt Lake that it had become my home in the wilderness.*

The men crossed the Jordan River by raft, then made their way north to Bear Lake. They arrived at the **rendezvous** on the 3rd of July, and there was much rejoicing because his friends thought he was dead.

Jedediah was a respected leader of other trappers. He was probably the first trapper to go all the way from the Mississippi River town of St. Louis to the California coast. He was the first to travel across Utah's length and width. He clearly showed that no rivers flowed from the Great Salt Lake into the Pacific Ocean.

Jedediah Smith explored much of Utah as he searched for beaver.

"My arrival caused a considerable bustle in camp, for myself and party had been given up as lost. A small cannon brought up from St. Louis was loaded and fired for a salute."

—*Jedediah Smith's diary, 1827*

Jedediah Smith and his men.
From a painting by Frederick Remington, a famous artist.

Provost Enters Utah Valley. **Provo and Orem are in Utah Valley today.**
(Painting by P. Salisbury)

James Baker in a beaver hat.

Etienne Provost was a French-Canadian who started trapping furs in New Mexico, but spent a lot of time in Utah. The City of Provo and the Provo River are named after him.

James Baker ran away from his childhood home in Illinois to become a trapper. Tall and slender, with long red hair, he liked wearing leather moccasins and leggings instead of store clothes. After trapping for several years in Utah, Colorado, and Wyoming, he married a Shoshone woman named Flying Dawn. Together they had fourteen children. When his trapping days were over, Jim became a scout for the Army. It was a good job for him, because he had traveled all over the land, knew the Indians, and knew where to find animals to hunt for food. At the time of his death he was a farmer in Wyoming.

Messages from the Past

Today, how can we know about mountain men? They lived more than 150 years ago, and they are not around for us to ask them questions. Here is one way.

In 1837 a French-Canadian trapper named **Antoine Robidoux** came up from New Mexico to trap in Utah. He carved a message in French on a rock in the Uintah Basin. Translated into English, it means: "Antoine Robidoux passed here November 13, 1837, to establish a house of trade at the Green or Uinta River."

Getting your picture taken by a photographer became quite popular during this period of time. Luckily for us, Jim Beckwourth, Jim Baker, and other trappers had their pictures taken at least one time in their lives. Beckwourth had his picture printed on cards so people back East could see what a real mountain man looked like. He gave the cards to people he met.

Another way we know about mountain men is that sometimes they kept diaries. **Osborne Russell** wrote this in his diary in 1835, when he was in the Utah Valley:

Robidoux inscription.

> *I passed the time as pleasantly at this place as ever I did among Indians. In the daytime I rode about the valley hunting waterfowl who rend the air at this season of the year with their cries.*

Russell also wrote about his Christmas holiday dinner near Ogden in 1840:

> *The first dish that came on was a large tin pan 18 inches in diameter rounding full of Stewed Elk meat. The next dish was similar to the first heaped up with boiled Deer meat The 3d and 4th dishes were equal in size to the first containing a boiled flour pudding prepared with dried fruit accompanied by 4 quarts of sauce made of the juice of sour berries and sugar. Then came the cakes followed by about six gallons of strong Coffee. . . . On being ready the butcher knives were drawn and the eating commenced at the word given by the landlady.*

How does this holiday meal compare with the ones at your house?

New Clothes

When a mountain man left a rendezvous, he usually had a complete outfit of new clothes. But by the end of the trapping season, these clothes were worn to rags and rotted from always being wet. During the winter when he couldn't trap, his wife made him new clothes out of leather. It was smoked nearly black, to make it as waterproof as possible. His moccasins were lined with fur for the winter. His wife often decorated his hunting shirt with porcupine quills or glass beads. He sometimes wore a blue cotton shirt under his hunting shirt. He wore either a wide-brimmed hat or a kind of turban made with a big blue bandanna. Sometimes he wore feathers in his hair.

Rendezvous

After mountain men had collected many beaver skins, they dug holes and hid them in the ground. Such a hole was called a *cache*. That is where the name of Utah's Cache County comes from. Mountain men cached many of their furs there.

Once a year the men brought their furs from the caches to a rendezvous. It was a big fair where they sold and traded the furs they had trapped during the year.

Rendezvous were a time of trading and socializing.
They were a lot like American Indian trade gatherings.

Furs sold for about $10 each. That would be more than $100 today. One trapper made $27,000 for the skins he had. The trappers also got the supplies they needed for the next year, like blankets, clothing, sugar, coffee, tobacco, knives, and bullets.

Besides trading, the mountain men also had a big party at their rendezvous. People ate, drank, and gambled. They had contests, horse races, shooting matches, and fights. They told stories about what had happened to them since they last met. Many Indians attended the rendezvous, too. Some of the rendezvous were held at Bear Lake. Others were held in the Cache Valley.

For men who often worked alone, the rendezvous was an important time.

Mountain Man Slang

Here is a list of words that mountain men used and what they meant. They are **slang** words.
Slang refers to things a group of people do or know about.

Buffler	Buffalo
Cache	Hiding place for furs, often a pit dug in the side of a mound
Critter	Animal
Pill	Bullet
Give 'em a teach	Teach them a lesson
Make beaver	Make money
Para swap	An even trade
Possibles sack	Sack of things to trade
Shining Mountains	Rocky Mountains
Vittles	Food
The way the stick floats	The way things happen. Today we might say, "The way the cookie crumbles."
Fixins	Things needed in the trapping business

Mountain Man Myth

Do you know what a **myth** is? It is something that many people believe, but it is more of a story than what really happened.

Some books tell us that mountain men were daring, brave, and tough. Supposedly, they fought Indians and bears and danger at every turn. They are said to have traveled alone, on foot, through terrible places. They faced hunger, storms, thirst, and accidents with great bravery. Mountain men did not hunt for money, we are told. They hunted because they loved danger, independence, and the thrill of wild lands.

That is the myth. It is only partly true. Here are some facts about mountain men:

- Many of the mountain men were married.
- Their wives and families often traveled with them.
- Many of them married American Indian women.
- Most of them trapped for a few years and then became guides, ranchers or farmers or store owners.
- They traveled by horse, mule, and canoe.
- Most died from old age. They lived longer than most Americans at the time.
- They made money trapping. Trapping was a business.
- They represented the *best* and the *worst* in people. They were brave, creative, and worked hard in a wild country. They were also greedy, violent, and **racist**.
- They often did not understand American Indians. Instead of respecting them, some saw them as people in the way. They said they were "obstacles to progress."

An **historian** tries to find the truth about the past. After learning the facts, go back and read the mountain man myth again. What parts of it are true? What parts are not?

What Shall We Name the Place?

Ashley Creek, Ashley Valley	Named for William Ashley, who was there in 1825
Bear River, Bear Lake	Named by English fur trapper Michel Bourdeau in 1819 because of the many bears there
Beaver (Town), Beaver County	Named for the many beavers in the area
Brown's Hole, on Green River, in Dagget County	Site of Fort Davy Crockett, built by mountain men
Cache Valley, Cache County	Named by Jim Beckwourth as his favorite place to cache furs; (formerly called Willow Valley)
Duchesne River, Duchesne (Town), Duchesne County	Named for French fur trapper, Du Chesne, who was in Uintah Basin about 1840
Henry's Fork, of the Green River	Named for Andrew Henry, partner of William Ashley
Logan, in Cache County	Possibly named for mountain man Ephraim Logan
Malad River, in Box Elder County	From the French malade, meaning sick; where some trappers got sick from eating beaver that had eaten poisonous roots
Ogden (City), Ogden River, Ogden Valley	Named for Peter Skene Ogden, trapper in the area in 1825
Provo (City), Provo River, Provo Canyon	Named for Etienne Provost, a trapper
Weber River, Weber Canyon, Weber County	Named for John H. Weber, a trapper

End of the Trapping Time

The mountain men were here for only about twenty years. By the early 1840s, their business was over. One reason was that beaver hats stopped being fashionable. They were a "fad" for a while, and then they were no longer very popular. Rich people began to want their hats made of shiny silk, not beaver. Also the beaver were almost extinct. The fur trappers had killed so many of them that only a few were left.

When the Mormons started settling in Utah in 1847, only one mountain man was still trapping in Utah. He was **Miles Goodyear**, and he built a trading post and house where the city of Ogden now is. He called it "Fort Buenaventura." It had a cabin, a garden, and corrals for his sheep and cattle.

There are still rendezvous at Fort Buenaventura today. People dress up like the old days, sell things they have made, have shooting contests, and live in the trapper style for a few days.

At a modern rendezvous people try to dress like mountain men did over 150 years ago.

Government Explorers

As the fur trade ended, the United States government started sending explorers to map the West. One of them was John C. Fremont. He led five expeditions to explore the western United States. Former mountain men, like Kit Carson, helped Fremont. Fremont made maps of the places he explored. He also wrote many reports about what the West was like. Pioneers used his reports as they planned their trips to the West.

During three of his trips Fremont came into Utah and spent a lot of time here. He and his men explored the Great Salt Lake and the area around it. They traveled along the Bear River and explored the Bear River Valley. They explored the area around St. George and Santa Clara. One of the people in the group was a black man named Jacob Dodson. During his life, Dodson was a hunter, boatman, soldier, and cowboy.

Every day Fremont took the temperature of the air. In his diary he wrote about the land, the soil, the plants and animals. He wrote about the American Indian people he met. Later his wife, Jessie Benton Fremont, helped him publish reports about his travels.

Fremont is remembered as the one who finally found a way west from the Salt Lake Valley to California. From the Great Salt Lake, he sent a scouting party across the barren

Fremont took readings of the stars at night. He also made maps and wrote about the places he explored for the government.

When he was an older man, John C. Fremont lived in California. He and his wife Jessie and daughter are in front of a giant California redwood tree.

salt flats. Their job was to find water and grass. About sixty miles away they could see a high mountain. They decided to ride toward the mountain and hoped to find water at its base. The group was to signal Fremont with smoke if they found it.

The next day Fremont led the rest of the men out onto the desert. When they camped, Fremont made his own fire signals to tell the scouting party where he was. Soon one of the scouts came into Fremont's camp. The scouting party had found water, grass for the horses, and wood. That afternoon, the whole group was at the base of the mountain. Fremont named it Pilot Peak, because it had guided them across the salt flats.

After Fremont finished exploring the western United States, he became interested in politics. He ran for president of the United States for the new Republican Party, but he was not elected.

Besides John Fremont, other explorers came to Utah. So did wagon trains of people on their way to California and Oregon. By the time Mormons came to Utah to make their home in 1847, many people had been here. A lot of people knew about Utah.

What Do You Think?

Discuss with your family at dinner tonight:

1. Is it right for a country to take natural resources from another country?

2. Is it right for people to try to change the lifestyle of other people?

3. How did the Domínguez-Escalante Expedition turn out to be important?

4. What were the best parts and the worst parts of a mountain man's life?

5. Did the mountain men have a right to kill so many beaver on land where the American Indians were living?

6. Should animals be killed so people can use their skin and fur for clothes?

Can You Remember?

1. Why did Spain want to colonize the Americas?

2. What was the reason for the Domínguez-Escalante Expedition?

3. Why did mountain men come to Utah?

4. What was beaver fur used for?

5. Jim Bridger started _____ in Wyoming.

6. Which trapper later became a businessman and opened stores at Fort Bridger and in Salt Lake City?

7. Who was a famous black mountain man?

8. Who almost lost his ear during the grizzly bear attack?

9. Who was the city of Provo named after?

10. John C. Fremont was sent by the United States government to _____ the West.

Geography Tie-In

1. Do beavers live where there are mostly forests and rivers, or deserts and basins? Why?

2. The mountain men did not have many maps. They made them as they explored. What is one reason they thought the Great Salt Lake was the Pacific Ocean?

Words to Know

colonize	myth
diary	racist
expedition	rendezvous
historian	slang

Handcart pioneers walked over the Mormon Trail to Utah.

A Long Journey –Moving to Zion

I n the 1840s many people in the East began moving west. They wanted to settle in California and Oregon. Thousands of people left their homes in other parts of the United States to start a new life. On their way to California and Oregon, some of those people passed through what we now call Utah. But they did not stay. They wanted a pleasant climate and fertile land where they could be farmers. Utah's land and climate seemed too harsh and dry to them.

In 1847, when it was still part of Mexico, a group of people moved to Utah. They were looking for a new place to live. They wanted to come here. After American Indians, they were the next people who wanted Utah as their home. They were the Mormons. In this chapter we will talk about them and their trip to Utah.

Who Were the Mormons?

"Mormon" was a nickname for people who belonged to a new church. They were called Mormons because they believed that a book called the *Book of Mormon* was the word of God, just as they believed the *Bible* was. The church's real name was, and is today, The Church of Jesus Christ of Latter-day Saints (or LDS Church for short). Joseph Smith was its first leader. The church had started in New York state in 1830. This was only a few years before Mormons began coming to Utah.

Most of the western settlers were on their way to the rich lands of Oregon and California. They passed over the dry Utah region.

The Homesteaders, painting by John Clymer ▶

Painting by Minerva Teichert ▶

Crossing the Mississippi on the Ice, painting by C.C.A. Christensen ▲

The Mormons had built the city of Nauvoo in Illinois. When they were forced to leave, it was winter. Luckily, the Mississippi River was frozen, which rarely happened. This made it easier for the wagons, animals, and people to cross into Iowa.

Mormons wanted to get other people to join their church. They wanted to **convert** them to what they thought was the true religion. They sent **missionaries** all over the United States and to other parts of the world to tell them about Mormonism. People joined the church. It grew rapidly. Soon it had thousands of members.

As more and more people became Mormons, they looked for a place to live together. They wanted to have what they called a "gathering place" where they could all be together. They wanted to build what they called "the Kingdom of God on Earth." They had problems, though. Wherever they went, many other people did not like them. They were always forced to move. They moved from New York to Ohio to Missouri, then to Illinois.

What was going on? Why didn't people like them? Mormons believed that their church was God's true church.

They believed that Joseph Smith was a prophet who talked to God. They wanted to build a perfect society where everyone would be equal and follow God. They wanted to share their possessions. These religious beliefs often upset people who were not Mormons.

There were also problems between Mormons and their neighbors over politics and land. The Mormons often all voted the same way. This gave them a lot of voting power. They also bought large pieces of land for farming. Their neighbors felt they were getting too powerful. Also, people heard that some Mormon men married more than one wife. This was called "polygamy." Polygamy really upset some people. (We will discuss this more in a later chapter.)

As a result, Mormons were driven out of some towns. Their crops were burned. So were their houses and barns. Their horses and cattle were stolen. People were hurt and killed in fights between Mormons and their neighbors. Finally anger reached such a pitch that a mob in Illinois shot and killed Joseph Smith and his brother, Hyrum Smith.

After that, Governor Ford of Illinois wrote a letter to Brigham Young, who was acting as the new leader of the church. Governor Ford said the Mormons were a peaceful, hard-working, and law-abiding people. But he could not promise them protection.

"If you can get off by yourselves, you might enjoy peace," the governor said, "not surrounded by such neighbors. I confess that I do not foresee the time when you will be permitted to enjoy quiet." He suggested that the Mormons move to California.

Brigham Young was the leader of the pioneers when they traveled to Utah.

To the Rocky Mountains

Finally, Mormons did decide to move far away from other people. They wanted to be alone where they could build their Kingdom of God without interference from other people. They thought about many places—California, Canada, and Texas. The place they finally chose was Utah. At that time it was not part of the United States. It was part of Mexico.

Mormons chose Utah for two reasons. First, it was **isolated**. It was a long way from other cities in the United States. They hoped they would be left alone and would not have trouble with their neighbors. Second, they chose Utah because the land was a hard natural environment. Other pioneers would pass it by and go on to California and Oregon.

Western Pioneer Trails

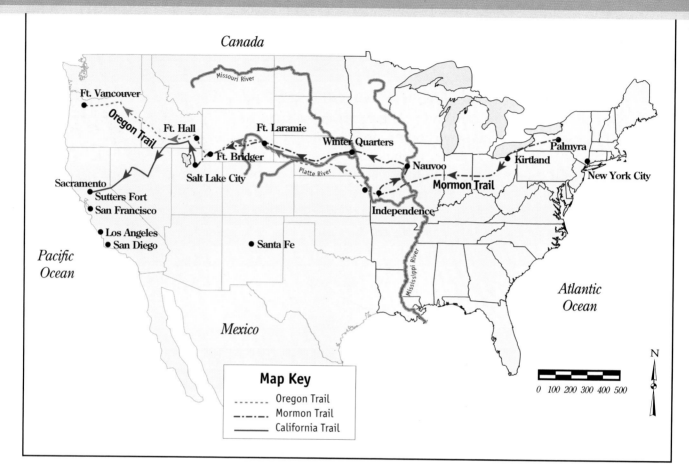

Map Key
- - - - - - Oregon Trail
- · - · - Mormon Trail
———— California Trail

Activity

The Mormon Trail

The Mormon pioneers mostly followed the path of other pioneer wagon trains that had gone to Oregon and California.

1. Which parts of the journey do you think would be the hardest?

2. Why did the Mormon Trail follow a river most of the way west?

3. When the pioneers left Illinois, they had to cross two large rivers. Which time of year would be easiest to cross a wide, deep river?

4. The Mormon pioneers wanted to be alone. Why do you think they decided to settle in the valley of the Great Salt Lake instead of going to Oregon or California?

Planning the Trip

Before they left the East, the people studied as much about Utah and the West as they could. They read reports of the fur trappers. They read guide books for people moving west. They read John C. Fremont's government report, and they took it with them to help them on the trip. It was kind of like a guidebook for them. They talked with as many people as they could who had been in the West.

Moving west took much planning. They could not just leave. Brigham Young was in charge of the journey. The pioneers were going to move more than 1,000 miles. They had to move about 15,000 people, 3,000 wagons, 30,000 cattle, and many mules and horses. It was not an easy job. They did not have cars, airplanes, or trains. There were only wagons and horses, mules, and oxen. And it would take a long time. They would not be able to travel very fast.

It was time to go West! "It was a day of excitement and apprehension, of fear and sorrow."

—*A member of the Advance Party*

Winter Quarters, by C.C.A. Christensen ▶

The pioneers traveled across Iowa to the banks of the Missouri River that first winter. They built cabins and waited for spring. 1846-47.

The First Two Pioneer Children

Isaac Kimball was only seven years old when he came to Utah. Later, after the people built a city and he grew older, the pony express came through the region. Isaac worked as a stable boy at pony express stations, taking care of the horses. He met the famous fur trappers, Kit Carson and Jim Bridger.

Lorenzo Kimball, who was only six when he came with the first group of pioneers, herded some of the first sheep in the Salt Lake Valley. After he and his parents helped settle Salt Lake City, he helped settle other towns in Utah.

"If the men of the church thought they were going out to some yonder place and pick a permanent abode for the women without even giving them the right of consultation, then they had some more guesses coming."

—*Harriet Wheeler Young*

Mormons had been living in Illinois, in a town they had built called Nauvoo. Nauvoo was next to the Mississippi River. When they had to leave, the first stop was a place in Iowa they called Winter Quarters. They built log cabins and camped there during the winter of 1846-47. It was a hard time. The weather was very cold. Sometimes there wasn't enough food, and they ate mainly cornmeal mush. Many people were sick. Some people died.

Ellen Kimball   Harriet Wheeler Young   Clarissa Decker Young
The first three Mormon pioneer women in Utah

The Advance Party

When spring came, the first group of pioneers left Winter Quarters and started west. They were headed for Utah. They were called an "advance party." Their job was to find a place and prepare the way for thousands of other people to settle. The day they left was a hard one. They had many different feelings. They were sad to leave their families. They were a little afraid, and they were excited.

The people packed their wagons with everything they thought they would need to get a new settlement started in Utah. They took seeds, plows, shovels, axes, and saws. They took clothes and blankets. They even carried a large leather fishing boat equipped with nets and fishing poles. They were not going just to look around or to hunt. They were going for the rest of their lives. They had to take everything needed to start life in a new place.

The advance group included 148 people. There were 143 men, 3 women, and 2 children. (When other groups came later, there were many more women and children.) There

The Wash is a painting by Gregory Sievers. Pioneers washed their clothes in rivers along the trail.

were 72 wagons, 93 horses, 52 mules, 66 oxen, 19 cows, 17 dogs, and some chickens. Brigham Young was the leader. The women were Clarissa Decker Young, Ellen Kimball, and Harriet Wheeler Young. The two children in the group were Ellen's two sons, Isaac and Lorenzo. Isaac was seven years old, and Lorenzo was six.

At first the advance group was going to be just men. Some men thought it would be too dangerous for women. That made some women mad.

The men, women, and children could walk only about fifteen miles a day, and sometimes less if the weather was bad. Some parts of the journey would be easier than others. They would be able to go the fastest at the first, when they were traveling along the flat plains of the Midwest. From Wyoming into Utah there were mountains, so it would be much harder and take longer.

The Salt Lake Valley at Last

It took the advance group three and a half months, more than one hundred days, to get to Utah. Mostly they traveled over a **route** other people had used on their way to California, along the Platte River. They arrived in the Salt Lake Valley on July 24, 1847. Ever since then, July 24 has been a holiday in Utah. Every city and town has some kind of celebration. There are rodeos, parades, fireworks, and community picnics.

"At evening after the chores were done, the pioneers would assemble around the campfire and Hans C. Hansen's violin would often be heard in the still night air, while a vocal selection would add to the merriment of the circle around the fire."

—*"Day by Day with the Utah Pioneers,"* Deseret News. *April 27, 1897*

African Americans Come to Utah

Three of the pioneers in the advance group were African American slaves. They were Hark Lay, Green Flake, and Oscar Crosby. Some books call them servants, but they were slaves. Other people in the group owned them as property. Their names are listed with the other pioneers on two monuments —the *Brigham Young Monument* in downtown Salt Lake City, and *This Is the Place Monument* at the mouth of Emigration Canyon.

This is an artist's drawing of Green Flake, who came into Utah with the advance company.

Of these three men, we know the most about Green Flake. Tradition says that he drove the wagon that brought Brigham Young into the valley. He was the slave of James M. Flake, a southerner who had lived in North Carolina and Mississippi. In 1843 James Flake and his family joined the Mormon church and moved to Nauvoo. He sold most of his slaves or gave them their freedom, but he kept Green, and also Liz, a young girl who was his wife's maid.

As the Mormon pioneers made preparations for the journey to Salt Lake in 1847, James Flake sent Green to help Brigham Young's pioneer company on the journey. He helped the pioneers plant crops and build houses. Then he returned east to help other Mormons leaving their homes to come west. He married Martha Crosby, and they became the parents of two children, Lucinda and Abraham. For a while Green Flake worked for Brigham Young. By 1860 he owned some land and was farming in the town of Union, in the southern part of the Salt Lake Valley. Later he moved to Idaho. When he died, his body was returned to Utah. He was buried next to Martha in the Union cemetery.

Green Flake and his wife and children lived in this home in the Salt Lake Valley.

After these first three men came to Utah, other black men and women came. Some were free, and some were slaves. Many Mormons did not believe people should own slaves. But some new converts had lived in southern states and already had slaves. When they left their homes, they brought their slaves with them to Utah. One group of pioneers who came during the second year included almost as many blacks as whites.

People by the Thousands

A few months after the advance group, more Mormon pioneers arrived in the valley. By the time winter began, there were nearly 2,000. And every year after that thousands more came. By the time the railroad came to Utah about twenty years later, more than 80,000 **immigrants** had come to Utah.

Painting by J. Leo Fairbanks ▶

View of the Salt Lake Valley
is a painting by J. Leo Fairbanks.

The Long Trip

Can you imagine what it was like to be one of the first pioneers? What would it be like to travel for months to get here? Let's see what the long trip to Utah was like before the railroad came. Many children who made the trip said it was hard, but it was also an adventure. See what you think.

Families traveled mostly with others in groups of wagons called **wagon trains**. The most common wagons were covered wagons. They were usually ordinary farm wagons with very heavy, sturdy wheels. They had canvas covers stretched over wooden frames to protect their loads. The wagons were like tents on wheels. From a distance they looked like small ships swaying across the wide plains. Their white canvas tops ballooned and whipped in the wind. Horses or oxen pulled them. Very small children rode in them. Mostly, though, the people walked beside them.

"The weather was hot, with a nice west wind blowing, but so dry that it parched the lips of the travelers."

—*"Day by Day with the Utah Pioneers,"* Deseret News. *April 27, 1897*

This is where thousands of pioneers left the Oregon Trail and went south into California.

"To enjoy such a trip . . . a man must be able to endure heat like a toad. . . . He must cease to think, except as to where he may find grass and water and a good camping place. It is a hardship without glory, to be sick without a home, to die and be buried like a dog."

—*An overlander to California, 1852*

Space had to be found in the wagon for everything they needed to bring—sacks, boxes, tools, furniture, bedding, clothes, and food. The heaviest items went in first and the lighter things on top. Food and cooking utensils were put where they could easily be reached every day. Women and children usually slept and dressed inside the wagons. The loads had to be arranged to leave level space for beds on top of the load. Often a space had to be made for a rocking chair for somebody's grandmother or grandfather to use.

Sometimes the last bit of space in the wagons had been filled, but necessary items were still lying on the ground. Then everything had to be unloaded. Families had to think again about what to leave behind and what to take. When there was not enough room for everything, some things were simply left by the side of the road. Sometimes other travelers picked them up.

Wagon trains started moving west in the late spring as soon as the prairies were green with grass for the livestock to eat. But too early a start meant a muddy trail. The early days of the trip were spent digging wagons out of the sticky mud.

A Daily Routine

Travelers soon established a daily routine. Brigham Young set out camp rules and everyone agreed to them. A bugle sounded at 5:00 in the morning to wake everyone up. They were on the road by about 7:00 and traveled until 6:00 or 7:00 at night.

Painting by Glen S. Hopkinson ▶

When the wagon train stopped for the night, the people camped with the wagons in a circle. Usually the camp was near a stream or a lake and trees. Guards kept watch all night, each man taking his turn. Everyone else was in bed by about 9:00. Many people slept in their wagons, but some also had tents and slept in them. Some just slept with blankets on the ground. Frequently before bedtime there was time to relax. People told stories, danced, sang, and played fiddles, banjos, and other musical instruments.

Joseph Fielding Smith traveled to Utah with his mother, Mary Fielding Smith. His father was Hyrum Smith, who had been killed in Illinois by an angry mob.

Working on the Trail

On the trail, everyone had a job to do. Men took care of the wagons and the animals. In the morning they hitched the teams to the wagons. All day long they carried their rifles and walked beside the wagons. At night, they drove the wagons into a circle and let the animals graze on the grass. Then they took turns guarding the stock, to prevent them from wandering away or being stolen.

The men did the hunting and fishing, too. Although people took food with them, it was not enough. They needed to kill animals along the way. The most common animals used for food were buffalo and antelope. Most people had never seen buffalo until then. Some days they saw thousands of them.

The travelers left messages on wooden markers along the trail about every ten miles. They were to help travelers who came along later. Some of the messages were long. Others were short. One just said, "All is well."

According to Thomas Bullock, a good breakfast consisted of "bacon, warm bread and light fried biscuits, and good coffee with sugar and milk."

Andrew Jenson wrote, "The pioneers found the buffalo herds numerous, and as deer, antelope, geese, ducks, etc., were still plentiful, the hunters would generally provide the whole camp with all the meat required."

It was the job of the men to fix whatever broke. And as the weeks wore on, more and more equipment needed repair. The men also had to push wagons out of ruts and up steep hills. Sometimes they had to get the wagons and cattle across deep rivers.

Women had different jobs. They were up first in the morning to make breakfast. Sometimes women called people to breakfast by singing out. The verse went like this:

Bacon in the pan,
Coffee in the pot,
Get up and get it,
Get it while it's hot.

Stopping along the trail to eat and rest.

During the day women rode in the wagons or walked, trying to keep a careful eye on their children. Lunch was usually only a brief stop for a cold meal. The real work for women came at night. Women cooked the evening meal and also lunch for the next day. There were no matches, so they had to keep striking with a flint and steel to get a spark. Whoever got her supper fire started first passed coals to her neighbors.

Some women began the trip ready to give birth. They had their babies along the trail. Sometimes the wagon train rested for a day after a birth. The recovering mother then rode in the rolling wagon with her new baby.

Younger children mostly stayed out of the way inside the wagons, while their older brothers and sisters walked and helped as much as they could.

Crossing the Rivers

Having to cross many rivers and streams caused the pioneers much trouble and endless delays. Sometimes wagons could just be driven across a stream. Often, though, the water was too deep. Then they could build rafts to get the wagons across while the animals swam. Or, instead, they could take the wagons off their wheels. They stuffed the cracks in the wagons with rags to make them as watertight as possible. Then the wagons floated across the river. A rope had been tied onto the front of each wagon and then stretched across the river. Men on the other side pulled on the ropes to bring the wagon across and keep it from being carried downstream.

It would usually take several days to get all of the wagons across a river. The advance party spent six whole days in June rafting and floating all of its wagons across a part of the Platte River.

"We carried our goods over on the raft, and we floated the wagons over by hand, assisted with ropes. But when the currents took them, the wagons would often roll over several times in the water and smash their bows. We also came near drowning our horses."

—*Early pioneer*

Crossing the many rivers was a real trial for the pioneers.
(Painting by Glen S. Hopkinson)

Buffalo Chips!

Children of all ages helped gather fuel. Finding enough dry wood for hundreds of cookfires was a problem. So what else do you suppose they could use for a fire?

This was buffalo country. The land was dotted with plate-sized, gray disks of dried buffalo dung. People called them buffalo chips. When they were broken into pieces, they burned very well and made a good fire. At first some people objected to handling or burning them. But soon it was common to see children darting to this side of the trail and that, gathering them up. They even had contests to see who could gather the most. Then they threw the buffalo chips into a canvas sheet slung like a hammock under the wagon.

Don't Get Hurt!

People often got sick. One of the most common illnesses was Rocky Mountain fever. They caught it from wood tick bites.

The trip to Utah was tiresome and exhausting. It could also be dangerous. On the trail there was no doctor to call and no ambulance to take people to the hospital. When someone broke an arm or leg, whoever had the nerve tried to help. Someone had to pull the limb straight and bind it with rough splints, while others held the person down. Then a place was made for the injured person to lie on bedding piled inside the wagon, and the train moved on.

Cuts and bruises were common. A cut was seldom sewn up. The wound was simply covered with tar, or lard (animal fat), or a mass of spider web, and tightly wrapped with a cloth. Another common way of treating a bad cut was to cover it with brown sugar before wrapping it.

Toothaches were common, too. If a mustard plaster did not reduce the swelling of an infected jaw, a pair of pliers was used to pull out the infected tooth. There was no anesthetic, except for whiskey. It was often used to kill germs and to deaden the pain. There was no aspirin or other drugs at that time.

One sick man, Erastus Snow, told about his "violent attack of mountain fever."

Within the week past about one-half of the camp has been attacked by the same complaint. [The sickness started out like a severe cold] producing soreness of the flesh and pains in the head and in all parts of the body; as the fever increases the pain in the back and head becomes almost insufferable, but an active portion of... [medicine], accom-

panied by warm and stimulating drinks, such as ginger and pepper, cayenne, etc., taken frequently . . . seldom fails to break it up, though it leaves the patient sore and feeble.

A major killer was a disease called cholera. It was spread by polluted water. The disease caused vomiting and diarrhea, which in turn led to death, often overnight.

The other major killer was accidents. There were drownings, accidental ax wounds, accidental shootings, and even children falling out of wagons and getting run over. In such cases, everyone helped each other. Orphaned children were taken in by other families.

People weren't the only ones who got hurt. Horses and cattle were often injured. One man in the advance party said, "A rifle went off by accident in John Brown's wagon. The ball went through a bag of clothes, which was set on fire, passed through the wagon and broke the fore-leg of a fine mare belonging to Stephen Markham. The bone was entirely severed. This made four of the best horses lost within the last four days."

This sculpture is of a father and mother who have just buried their child along the trail to Utah.

Pesky Insects

Mosquitoes and buffalo gnats were an awful problem. From still pools of water along the streams, the mosquitoes rose in clouds. They attacked every inch of exposed flesh on people and animals. They even covered the hides of horses and cattle, driving them frantic. Travelers learned to sit around small smudge fires of green sage whenever possible, because the smoke helped keep the insects away. But the fires were of no use to people doing their camp chores or walking on the trail during the day. At night the only escape was to burrow underneath the blankets, no matter how hot it was.

Buffalo gnats, while smaller than mosquitos, were almost as bad. During the day they hung in clouds in front of people and animals, getting into their eyes, nostrils, and ears.

Sometimes the trail would lead through country heavily infested by grasshoppers and crickets. They did not bite or sting, but they continually flew up and landed on people's clothes and in their hair. They got into everything—cooking pots, skillets, water buckets, eating utensils, bedding. They made eating and sleeping very unpleasant.

One man said, "The ground seemed to be alive with large crickets. A person who had never seen them could form no idea of the vast number of crickets in this region. The ground was almost covered with crickets."

Handcarts Across the Trail

For a few years some groups of Mormon pioneers pushed and pulled two-wheeled carts, called handcarts, loaded with their belongings. Altogether more than 3,000 people came to Utah that way.

Mary Ann Hafen was a child in 1860 when she went to Utah with the last handcart company. "There were five to our cart," she remembered. "Father and Mother pulled it; Rosie (two years old) rode; John (nine) and I (six) walked. When it was downhill, they let me ride, too. . . . Mother's feet were so swollen that she could not wear shoes, but had to wrap her feet with cloth."

Once Mary Ann's father decided to hitch one of the cows to the cart to pull it. It got scared and started running as fast as it could. The cart turned over. The children were all riding in it. They fell out and were cut and bruised. After that, their father always pulled the cart himself.

Painting by Clark Kelley Price ▲

Some pioneer men, women, and children died along the trail. The Martin Handcart Company left late in the summer, and didn't reach Utah before the snow caused great suffering and many deaths.

What Do You Think?

There are some important things to think about in this chapter!

1. Do we have the right in America to join any religion we want to, or join none at all?

2. What could help us be more tolerant of people who believe differently than we do?

3. Can you think of other groups in history who have moved to new places so they could live their religion without being persecuted?

4. There are many different kinds of persecution. Talk about what it means. Talk about why we should try to treat other people fairly.

5. What would you have disliked about the trip to Utah? What would you have liked?

Can You Remember?

1. Where in the West were pioneers who were not Mormons going?

2. Why did the Mormons want to move west?

3. What was the journey like? Think of five words to describe it.

4. What were some of the dangers the pioneers faced?

5. How long did it take a wagon train to travel to Utah?

6. What were five things the pioneers took with them?

Geography Tie-In

1. Look at the map on page 80. Which of today's states did the Mormon Trail go through?

2. As a class, draw on the board a large map like the one in the book. Put mountains on it. Put the largest rivers on it. Draw the trail on it. Compare the distance of the plains to the distance over the mountains. Which is farther? Which would be harder to cross?

3. What things in nature (weather, landforms, animals, plants) helped the pioneers? What things in nature made the trip even harder?

Words to Know

convert

immigrant

isolate

missionary

route

wagon train

One of the first things pioneers
did was dig ditches to bring
water to the crops.

chapter 6

Settling the Salt Lake Valley

There is a myth about the Salt Lake Valley. It says that the valley was a **barren** and lifeless desert with only one tree when the first Mormon pioneers arrived. The painting on the left shows the valley this way, with only one tree.

Orson F. Whitney, an early writer, described the valley this way:

> *. . . a broad and barren plain hemmed in by mountains, blistering in the burning rays of the mid-summer sun . . . on all sides a seemingly interminable waste of sagebrush bespangled with sunflowers—the paradise of the lizard, the cricket, and the rattlesnake. . . .*

Whitney's language is wonderful. It sounds like poetry. But is that how the Salt Lake Valley really was?

William Henry Jackson, an artist, also described the valley with paint. Look carefully at his painting on the next page. It shows the Mormon pioneers first looking at the valley. What does it look like? Does it look like a dry desert with no water? Do you see any plants, bushes, or trees? Are there any streams in the painting? What grows near streams? Was the valley a forest? Would it be possible to farm?

Do you live in the Salt Lake Valley, or have you ever been there? There are mountains on both sides of the valley. On the east are the Wasatch Mountains. Seven streams run out of the mountains into the valley. Does it make sense that there would be no trees growing?

A newly arrived family builds their first log home with the help of neighbors.

Great Salt Lake Valley is a painting by William Henry Jackson.

> Trees and bushes grew along all of the streams that flowed from the mountains to the Jordan River and into the Great Salt Lake. On the mountains were forests of pine trees.

Here is what the valley was really like when Mormon pioneers first came. Much of it had rich, good soil. Wherever sagebrush grows, the soil is good, and sagebrush grew all over the valley. There were also tall grasses. Trees and bushes grew along all of the streams that flowed from the mountains to the Jordan River and into the Great Salt Lake. On the mountains were forests of pine trees.

How do we know this today? We can learn much about the past from diaries of people who lived then. Here is part of a diary written by Thomas Bullock. He was one of the first Mormon pioneers to enter the Salt Lake Valley:

> *As we progressed down the valley small clumps of dwarf oak and willows appear, the Wheat grass grows 6 or 7 feet high, many different kinds of grass appear, some being 12 or 13 feet high—after wading thro' thick grass for some distance, we found a place bare enough for a camping ground, the grass being only knee deep, but very thick; we camped on the banks of a beautiful little stream; which was surrounded by very tall grass.* —July 22, 1847

What did you learn about the Salt Lake Valley from Bullock's diary?

Most people were happy with the way the valley was. Some liked it better than others did. In his diary, Wilford Woodruff called it a "vast, rich fertile valley . . . clothed with the heaviest garb of green vegetation in the midst of which lay a large lake of salt water . . . abounding with the best fresh water springs, rivulets, creeks, brooks, and rivers of varied sizes."

Orson Pratt noticed, however, that "the grass had nearly dried up for want of moisture" and that "the drier places were swarming with very large crickets, about the size of man's thumb."

Others were downright unhappy. Harriet Young wanted to go on to California: "Weak and weary as I am, I would rather go a thousand miles further than to remain in such a forsaken place as this," she said. Her daughter added that the other women of the party also "felt a sense of desolation and loneliness—in the new country to which they had come." Clarissa Decker Young said, "I cried, for it seemed to me the most desolate place in all the world."

Making a Home in the Valley

The Salt Lake Valley is large. The first thing the group had to do was find a camping place. They could have camped anywhere they wanted to in the whole valley. Where do you suppose they did? What kind of place would they choose?

They wanted to be near water, of course. They camped near one of the streams that flowed into the Salt Lake Valley. They named it City Creek. They camped near it where the City and County Building is now.

This is Salt Lake City in 1858, 11 years after the first pioneers reached the valley of the Great Salt Lake.

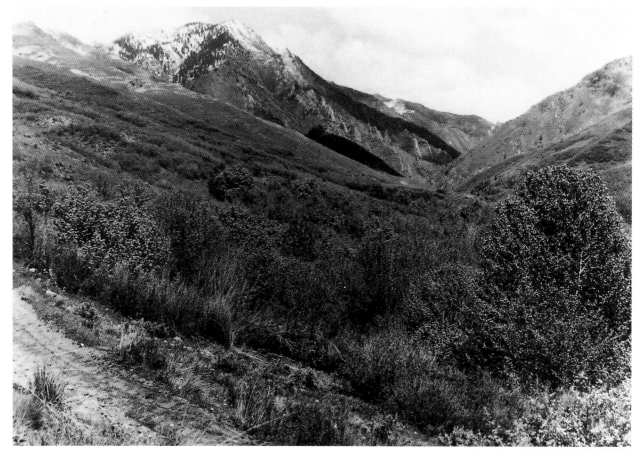

City Creek flows down this canyon into the Salt Lake Valley.

Activity
What Would You Do First?

Join with a group of classmates. Suppose you are part of the first group of Mormon pioneers to arrive in the Great Salt Lake Valley. You have ridden in wagons and walked more than 1,000 miles to get here. Now it is time to make the valley your home.

You must help get it ready for thousands of other people who will come to join you. People will live here for a long time.

1. What will you have to do? Make a list. Put the most important things first, then the next, and so on.

2. Compare your list with the lists of other groups. Did your group forget anything?

3. Which group in your class has the best chance to start a successful settlement?

Now compare your list with what the Mormon pioneers actually did. See how good of a pioneer you would have made.

Getting the Work Done

The work of the first settlers of Salt Lake City was important. Later when people founded other cities and towns in Utah, they did the same things.

They decided to **cooperate**. They organized people into groups to do jobs. They worked together instead of letting each person do whatever he or she wanted. Everyone worked for the common good. Each family took care of itself and also helped others. Salt Lake was not settled by separate individuals, but by people working together.

When they came to Utah, the Mormons wanted to show the rest of the world that cooperation could work. Brigham Young said, "Each will put his mite [small part] together for that which is the best for every man, woman, and child."

Cutting Timber for Homes

One group went to the mountains to cut **timber**. They went first to City Creek Canyon, and then to Red Butte Canyon, and then to the canyon that led them into the valley. They named it Emigration Canyon.

"Brother George A. Smith took his ax and began chopping at a dry pole, and after hitting a few licks, the top flew off and hit him on the head hard enough to knock him down. That put an end to his chopping timber for a living."

—*John Steele*

The pioneers had to go into the nearby mountains to cut trees for homes.
They carried the logs down into the valley on wagons pulled by horses or oxen.

Exploring the Valley

Another group explored the valley. They climbed to the top of Ensign Peak to have a good look around. When they climbed down, they found a hot spring and bathed in it. They traveled to the Great Salt Lake to see what it was like and to gather salt. The men brought back twelve bushels of coarse salt and one barrel of "fine, white table salt."

They went swimming in the lake. Wilford Woodruff later wrote in his diary that "No person could sink in it, but would roll and float on the surface like a dry log." He thought the lake was one of the "wonders of the world."

Hunting and Farming

A group was organized to go out to hunt and fish. They did not have very good luck, though. In eight days they killed only one rabbit, one badger, one wolf, three sage hens, and four fish.

Working in teams, the pioneers plowed the land and planted crops. They needed to have food for winter. They planted corn, oats, potatoes, wheat, beans, and even turnips. The land was so dry they had to do what the American Indians had done in the past. They had to irrigate. They dug a ditch from City Creek to carry water onto the crops they had planted. The crops were in the middle of what is now downtown Salt Lake City. Some of the crops were about where the Crossroads Mall is now.

Building Homes

The pioneers also built their homes. They decided to live close together. Instead of each family living somewhere separately, they built their log cabins inside a fort. They made the walls of the fort with **adobe** bricks.

SOUTH FORTS   NORTH FORT

The first cabins were built in a fort. This drawing shows how it might have looked.

To make the bricks, they mixed wet clay or mud with straw or plants. Then they molded the mud and straw mixture into bricks and dried them in the sun. Inside the walls, they built their cabins out of logs. By winter they had 423 cabins. They kept their cattle inside the fort, too. It was located where Pioneer Park is today.

This is a painting of the first homes in Provo. They were built touching each other to make the outside walls of the fort.

Being Self-sufficient

The pioneers built sawmills to cut lumber and gristmills to grind wheat into flour. They built blacksmith shops to repair tools and make horseshoes, nails, and tools. They built factories to make glass and hats and boots. They wanted to produce everything they needed.

Brigham Young said, "We do not intend to have any trade or commerce with the gentile [non-Mormon] world, for so long as we buy of them, we are . . . dependent upon them." Mormons, he said, needed to "produce, manufacture, and make every article of use . . . among our own people."

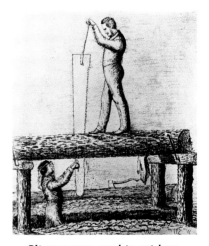

Pit saws were used to cut logs. One person stood down in a pit and helped move the saw up and down.

Mormon Villages

Manti

When other cities and towns were founded in Utah, they were also laid out the way Salt Lake City was. Salt Lake provided a model for the settlers of other towns to follow. Historians called these towns Mormon villages. Can you find the wide streets in a square pattern in these photographs of Manti and St. George? Can you find the temples?

St. George

Planning the City

The founders of Salt Lake City planned carefully. They gave their new city a name. They called it the Great Salt Lake City of the Great Basin, North America.

It was modeled on a plan Joseph Smith had used in other cities founded by Mormons, before they came to Utah. Salt Lake was not going to be a typical American city. It would look like a Mormon city.

The city was shaped like a big rectangle. There was no business district. In the city center was a site for a temple. Some people called it a "Temple City." Streets were very wide (132 feet). So were sidewalks (20 feet).

Streets did not wind around. They went straight and went north and south and east and west. The streets were not named for presidents, other people, or trees, as in some cities. They were named for their distance and direction from the temple. For example, 4th South Street was the fourth street south of the temple, and 6th East Street was the street six blocks east of the temple.

Home lots were large so that each family would have room for a garden and cows and other animals. Houses were to be set back on the lot, not too close to the street. Houses were not to face directly across the street from each other. One family's house would face another family's garden. Brigham Young told them, "Every man should cultivate his own lot and set out every kind of fruit and shade tree and beautify the city."

> "There shall be no private ownership of the streams that come out of the canyons, nor the timber that grows on the hills. These belong to the people; all the people."
>
> —*Brigham Young*

Compare this early photograph with the one of Salt Lake City today on page 164. What things are different?

This is the earliest known photograph of Salt Lake City, taken in 1854. This was seven years after the city was started. It shows the straight, wide streets. Do you know why it doesn't show the Mormon Temple?

The streets in the new city were said to be "wide enough to turn a wagon around in."

"Build good houses, school houses, meeting houses, and other public buildings, fence gardens and plant out fruit trees that Ogden might be a permanent city."

—*Brigham Young, 1849*

Besides the temple block, three other blocks were set aside as public squares. Houses or businesses would not be built on them. The idea was that they would be like islands in the middle of the busy city where people could go to relax. They would belong to everyone. The *Deseret News* called them "places of public resort, breathing spots, to be beautiful and adorned."

Beyond the city was farm land called "the big field." It was divided into small, medium, and large plots. People were to live in town and drive out to their fields each day for work. The purpose was to have people live close to each other and to their leaders.

Everyone Owned the Land

Early on, people decided what the land policy would be for the new settlement. People would not make a profit by selling land. Land would belong to the whole community, and it would be given to people for free. They would not have to buy it. How much land people got would not depend on who they were, or who they knew, or how much money they had. It would depend on what they needed.

People with large families would get more land than people with small families or unmarried people. After they were given land, people were not to sell it. And they would keep it only as long as they needed it and used it. If they didn't need it, it could be taken from them and given to someone else who truly did need it. The exact location of a person's land was decided by drawing numbers out of a hat.

The same thing applied to all natural resources. No one person was to own water, timber, or coal deposits. Those were to be used by all the people.

The Mormon pioneers didn't want some people to be poor and some to be rich. They wanted everyone to be equal. People should have only as much money as they needed.

A New Government

The people set up a government and made laws. The first government was different from the kind in other territories or states. It was not a **democracy**, in which voters hold the ruling power. Neither were church and government separated.

Instead, the people set up a **theocracy**. That meant that Mormon church leaders were also government leaders. The Mormon church's High Council was in charge. It passed laws. It carried out laws. It tried cases of breaking the laws.

Here are some of the laws that were passed.

1. Dogs could not run loose at night. The fine for not obeying the law was from one to five dollars. If a dog was a pest, it could be killed.
2. Every person had to have a job. No one could be idle. If people could not find jobs, the community would find one for them.
3. People could not disturb the peace.
4. People could not break the Sabbath.
5. Businessmen could not charge high prices for their goods and services. They could not take advantage of their customers.
6. After they moved onto their land, the people had to plant shade trees.
7. The following things were against the law:

   drunkenness
   stealing
   destroying property
   cursing, swearing
   unnecessary firing of guns
   making too much noise
   storing too much timber for fuel
   letting livestock run loose

Being drunk, disturbing the peace, and making too much noise were all against the law in early Salt Lake City.

A marshall enforced the laws. He arrested people, and he made sure they were punished if found guilty. At first there were no jails, so there had to be other punishments. One punishment was to pay a fine. Another punishment was to be whipped on the bare back, up to thirty-nine lashes. This hardly ever happened, however.

The First Winter in the Salt Lake Valley

The weather that first winter was mild and pleasant. Even so, life was not easy for people.

Crops need to be planted in the spring to have time to grow. The pioneers did not arrive here until late July. Even though they planted crops the very first day, it was late in the summer. Most of the crops the pioneers planted that first summer did not grow. That first winter there were no vegetables, and only a little flour to make bread. Sometimes they killed a cow for meat.

In his diary Lorenzo Dow Young wrote about how hungry his family became. They even made soup from the skin of a cow: "To prepare a meal, a piece of the skin was boiled in water until it became a glue soup, when salt was added."

Utes and Shoshones lived in the valleys to the north and south of the pioneers. They taught the settlers how to dig for the roots of plants that were fit to eat. The bulb of the sego lily was a favorite. Today the sego lily is Utah's state flower.

The bulbs of sego lilies and thistles helped keep people alive.

Seagulls and Crickets

The next spring people planted their crops. When the seeds they had planted began to come up from the ground as young plants, frost destroyed many of them. Then large numbers of crickets came and began eating the plants. The crickets were one thing the people noticed when they first came to the Salt Lake Valley and began to look around. William Clayton said, "The ground seems literally alive with very large black crickets crawling around up grass and bushes." One woman said this in a diary:

Today to our utter astonishment, the crickets came by millions, sweeping everything before them. They first attacked a patch of beans for us and in twenty minutes there was not a vestige [any] of them to be seen. They next swept over peas, then came into our garden; took everything clean.

The crickets ate so many plants that some people thought they would not be able to grow enough food to eat. They talked about moving to California. People fought the crickets in many ways. They banged on tin pans to scare them away. They knocked them off the plants with branches and brooms. They gathered them up in large baskets and burned them or dumped them in the river.

**Seagulls ate thousands of crickets.
The pioneers believed they came
as an answer to prayer.**
(Painting by Jack Vigos)

Seagulls helped destroy the insects. They flew in flocks from the nearby Great Salt Lake and ate thousands of crickets. A man named John Smith wrote to Brigham Young to tell him about the help the seagulls had given them. He said, "The crickets are still quite numerous, but between the gulls and our own efforts and the growth of our crops, we shall raise much grain in spite of them. Our vines, beans, and peas are mostly destroyed by frost and the crickets, but many of us have more seed and are now busy replanting."

For many years after that seagulls returned to farmers' fields, eating crickets, grasshoppers, worms, and other insects. In 1913 the Seagull Monument was built on Temple Square in Salt Lake City. In 1955 the Utah State legislature named the seagull the Utah state bird.

Heavy snow the second winter made life hard. In the mountains it almost buried a cabin.

The Second Winter

The first winter was hard for people, but the weather was mild. The second winter was different. It came early and was **severe**. Temperatures were often below zero, and it snowed all the time. Firewood was hard to find. No one starved, but no one gained weight either. People ate whatever they could find—rawhide, sego lily roots, and thistles.

"I used to eat thistle stalks," one person remembered, "until my stomach would be as full as a cow's." More and more families ate "glue soup" like Lorenzo Young's family did.

In response to the hard times, once again the people cooperated. Instead of leaving each family alone to figure out what to do, the church leaders asked people to share their food with everyone else. However, some people were not sure they wanted to do that. That made Brigham Young angry. He said, "If those that have do not give to those that have not, we will just take it and distribute it among the Poors, and those that have and will not share willingly may be thankful that their Heads are not found wallowing in the Snow."

The first years in Utah were hard, but most people worked together to solve problems. After a few years the valley had cities and farms. People from many countries worked together in their new home.

What Do You Think?

1. In what ways did the Mormon pioneers cooperate to build Salt Lake City?

2. When they first saw it, some people thought the Salt Lake Valley looked wonderful. Others were very disappointed when they saw it. What might be some reasons the people thought differently? Do people today think about a place the same way?

3. Do you think it would be easy for the people to cooperate all of the time? What were some good things about it? What might be some problems?

4. After working so hard to get to the Valley, how do you think the people felt when they had such a hard winter after they got here?

Can You Remember?

1. Was the Salt Lake Valley a desert when the pioneers first came? Explain.

2. How was the city laid out?

3. Why were there public squares in Salt Lake City?

4. How did people in Salt Lake City get land?

5. How did people in Salt Lake City make it through the first winter?

Geography Tie-In

1. What things in nature did the people use that first year in the Salt Lake Valley?

2. How did the people change the land once they got here?

3. Talk about some of the things that were moved here from other places: people, things, ideas.

Words to Know

adobe
barren
cooperate
democracy
severe
theocracy
timber

Groups of people traveling west stopped in Utah towns, then moved on. New Mormon immigrants came by the thousands. They often stayed a short time, then moved to settle other Mormon towns.

Branching Out Across the Land

What happened after Salt Lake City was firmly established? Many things were going on. Thousands of people kept coming every year. They started new cities and towns. As this happened, Mormons and American Indians came into contact with each other. Often there was conflict. Eventually the Indian lifestyle was changed forever here, just as it was in other parts of the United States. We will talk about these things in this chapter.

The Forty-Niners

Gold was discovered in California just one year after the pioneers first came here. In 1849 thousands of people passed through Utah on their way to California. They hoped to find gold and strike it rich. They were called forty-niners.

The forty-niners often arrived in Utah with tired animals, broken wagons, and little food. They needed to stop, repair their wagons, and rest before going on for 800 more miles. Most of them moved on, but some stayed.

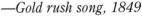

Ho! To California
We've formed our band
   and are well mann'd
To journey afar
   to the promised land,
Where the golden ore
   is rich in store,
On the banks of the
   Sacramento shore.
Then ho! Brothers ho!
   To California go.
There's plenty of gold
   in the world we're told,
On the banks of the
   Sacramento.
Heigh O, and away we go,
Digging up gold in
   Francisco.

—*Gold rush song, 1849*

Fanny and Julius Brooks were Jewish immigrants. They came to Utah and opened a hat store and bakery.

Samuel Auerbach opened a store that sold everything from saddles to clothes.

The Kahn brothers, Samuel and Emanuel, also opened a store in early Salt Lake City. They helped build the first Jewish synagogue.

Store Owners and Soldiers

People started coming to Utah to open stores. The first businessmen in Salt Lake, James Livingston and Charles Kinkead, were not Mormons. They opened the first store on Main Street, where the Crossroads Mall is now.

Other businesspeople followed. Some of them were Jewish, like Fanny Brooks and her husband, Julius; the Auerbach brothers and the Kahn brothers. Soon Jewish religious services were held in Salt Lake City.

Government officials and their families also arrived. Soldiers came. The first two forts they established were Camp Floyd and Camp Douglas. We will read more about these soldiers later.

Stores and businesses in Salt Lake City were opened by Jewish immigrants.

Soldiers from the United States Army came to Salt Lake City.

Immigration

Every year after Salt Lake City was founded, thousands of people arrived in Utah. This is called immigration. For a while, most of the people who came were Mormons. A child could grow up here and hardly ever know a person who was not a Mormon.

Church leaders sent missionaries all over the United States and the world to convert people to Mormonism. When people joined the Mormon church, they usually moved to Utah. Utah was the "gathering place."

How did so many Mormon converts travel to Utah? If they lived outside the United States, they came to this country by ship. Sometimes they landed in New Orleans and traveled up the Mississippi River to St. Louis. Then they traveled to Utah by wagon train. Sometimes their ship stopped in New York City. Then they traveled to St. Louis by train, and then to Utah by wagon train.

"Come to the Place of Gathering, Even in Flocks, as Doves Fly to Their Windows Before a Storm."

—*Brigham Young, 1852*

Painting by Glen Hopkinson ▶

New converts to the Mormon church traveled in large groups to Utah.
This mother and her children are leaving England on a ship.

March 2:

The last three days have been a succession of exceedingly heavy storms. . . . It is awful, but grand, to look upon the sea. I could only compare it to the boiling of an immense cauldron covered with white foam, while the roaring of the winds and waves was like the bellowing of a thousand wild bulls.

—*from Jean Rio Baker's diary*

Most immigrants did not come alone. They came in large groups with their families and with other Mormons. The Mormon church had an organized plan to help people move to Utah. Church leaders in Europe rented ships for immigrants to travel on.

A Ship from Denmark

Christian A. Madsen traveled on a ship from Denmark. More than four hundred people were on it. Some things about the trip were good, he said, and some things were hard. He liked the food: "sweet soup on Sundays, peas on Monday, rice mush on Tuesday and Wednesday, peas on Thursday, barley mush on Friday, fish and potatoes on Saturday." Everything was kept clean and sanitary. "The deck was washed three times a week and twice during the journey the ship was disinfected with smoked tar."

There was also time for fun, Mr. Madsen wrote: "We danced nearly every day on the ship. Some of the brethren and sisters had their music and would play for the dances. So we had very pleasant times." Mormon adults often called each other brother and sister, even if they weren't related.

A hard time came when many people on the ship got sick with the measles. "The sick got weak, lost their appetite for the biscuits, but later they learned to soak them in water for eight or twelve hours and that made them more like the Danish sister bread," Mr. Madsen said. "Nearly everyday pancakes were cooked by the hundreds for the sick and those who didn't like biscuits. Very often we baked wheat bread for the old folks who couldn't chew the hard ship bread."

Starting New Towns

About 100,000 Mormons had arrived in Utah by the year 1900. Most of them came from countries in Europe; half of them were from Great Britain. Most of the rest were from other countries in Europe, such as Denmark, Sweden, France, and Switzerland. Others came from Canada.

New immigrants usually stayed for the winter in Salt Lake City. With the arrival of spring most moved to other cities and towns and settled there.

In the first ten years, the immigrants founded more than one hundred towns. By the end of twenty years, they had founded over two hundred towns. By the end of the 1800s, when Utah became a state, they had founded nearly five hundred cities and towns.

Immigrants from Europe

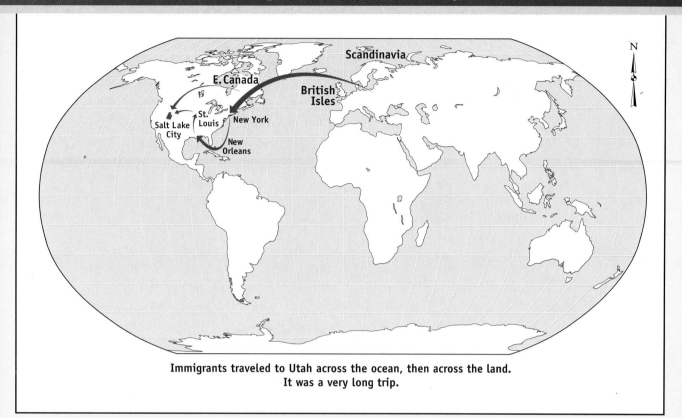

Immigrants traveled to Utah across the ocean, then across the land.
It was a very long trip.

Life was hard on a ship. It was crowded, and the people often got sick.

Spreading Out

New places were often settled when people decided by themselves to move somewhere else. Most places in the Salt Lake Valley were settled this way.

Why didn't the immigrants just stay in the Salt Lake Valley? If you think about it, you know the answer from what we have already studied.

First, thousands of people were coming every year from all over the world. They needed room. Other valleys would have to be found and settled. Second, Mormons wanted to be **self-sufficient**. They wanted to grow their own food and make everything they needed. Some settlements could supply what others needed. St. George would produce cotton, grapes, and sugar. Cedar City would start mining iron. Coalville would mine coal.

A number of families, led by John Holladay, established a farming community on Big Cottonwood Creek. They called it Holladay and built cabins close together in a village. Soon there were also settlements called East Mill Creek, Big Cottonwood, South Cottonwood (Murray), Sugar House, West Jordan, Granger, Taylorsville, and Draper. Mostly these were near streams.

People first went north from Salt Lake City in search of pastures for their cattle. Perrigrine Sessions and Hector C. Haight spent the winter of 1847-48 there. They found rich soil, with water available. So they encouraged other people to come. Soon people had founded the towns of Bountiful, Farmington, Kaysville, and Layton.

Immigrants often left Salt Lake City and went to other places in Utah to start farms. Some became very prosperous. This is the Bennion Farm, outside of Salt Lake City, painted by an immigrant from Norway.

Painting by Weggeland ▲

Called to Settle a New Town

Other people did not just go to a new place on their own. They went because Mormon church leaders "called" them to settle in a new place and help start a new town. A "call" meant it was a person's religious duty to go.

Dale Morgan reported these examples of church callings:

> *This group from Denmark should go to the Sanpete Valley, where they would feel at home in the considerable Scandinavian colony already established there. These Swiss would go to the Rio Virgin Valley where they too would feel at home. This brother or sister should go to Fillmore, where good blacksmiths were much needed now. This sister should go to St. George, where her knowledge of cotton growing perhaps would find a field of abundant usefulness.*

Settling St. George

In 1861 a list of 309 people was read in the Mormon church's general conference. They were to go with Erastus Snow and George A. Smith to set up a new town. They called it St. George. Because the weather was so warm there, and they grew cotton, it was often called Utah's Dixie.

"It is expected," Brigham Young said, "that the brethren will become permanent settlers in the southern region; that they will cheerfully contribute their efforts to supply the territory with cotton, sugar, grapes, tobacco, dates, almonds, olive oil and such other articles, as the Lord has given us the places for garden spots in the south to produce."

When Brigham Young called people to settle a new place, he expected that they would. "When the First Presidency ordered a thing," he said, "they need not ask questions but just do as they were told."

**St. George was named after George A. Smith.
He is the man with the white beard in the center of the picture.**

"This news was very
unexpected to me. . . .
I had a good home,
and plenty to do.
But when the Apostle
George A. Smith told me
I was selected to go,
I saw the importance of
the mission. . . .
We go with joy, leaving
our happy home, which
had cost about four years
of hard work. . . ."

—*John Pulsipher*

Some people were happy to go. Others had mixed feelings. One person wrote a song about what he thought. Here are two verses from it.

Oh, once I lived in Cottonwood, owned a little farm.
But I was called to Dixie, which gave me much alarm.
To raise the cane and cotton, right away I must go,
The reason why they sent me, I am sure I do not know.

I yoked old Jim and Bally up, all for to make a start,
To leave my home and garden, it almost broke my heart.
We moved along quite slowly, and always looked behind,
For the sands and rocks of Dixie, kept running through my mind.

Elijah Averett told how his father came home after a hard day in the fields to learn that he had been called to Utah's Dixie. At first he dropped in his chair and said he wouldn't go. Then after sitting a few minutes with his head in his hands, he stood up, stretched, and said, "Well, if we are going to Dixie, we had better start to get ready."

Some people were called to settle two or three or four different places during their lifetimes. If their services were needed somewhere else, Brigham Young did not hesitate to "call" them again.

This is St. George in 1910. What do you see in the picture that lets you know the time is later than when the pioneers first settled there?

American Indians and Pioneers

Salt Lake City and other Utah towns were settled mostly by people from Europe. It is important to remember, however, that the pioneers did not move onto empty land. The land in 1847 was not just a wilderness waiting to be filled up with people. Other people lived here. Utah was their home. Historians think that between 20,000 and 35,000 American Indians were already living in Utah when the pioneers came.

What happened between the two groups of people?

There were no problems between the pioneers and Indians as long as the new settlers stayed in the Salt Lake Valley. No Indian people lived there. But soon Mormons began to move onto land that was already occupied by the Indian people.

> "All of Utah's towns sit on archaeological sites. This means that almost every town in Utah today is in a place where Indian people were living when the new settlers came."
>
> —*David Madsen, Archaeologist*

Ute Indians lived the closest to Salt Lake City. They are lined up in front of the ZCMI department store in 1869.

Little Soldier, a Northwestern Shoshone, was baptized a member of the Mormon Church. A speaker at his funeral said, "He was a peaceful, honest, . . . man, and was always a welcome guest at the houses of many people in this county [Weber County]."

One of the first areas settlers moved to outside of Salt Lake was Utah Valley, where Provo is today. A large group of Utes already lived there, around Utah Lake. They did not want other people moving onto their land. When Mormon settlers moved into Sanpete Valley, they found many Utes also living there. When settlers moved into Cache Valley, they found Shoshones. And in Tooele Valley they found Goshutes. In fact, almost every place Mormon settlers moved they found American Indians.

"The watering places are all occupied by the white man. The grass that product mutch seed is all et out. The sunflowere seed is destroyed in fact thare is nothing for them to depend upon but beg or starve."

—*Jacob Hamblin, 1880*

Many Indian children died from measles and smallpox. They got the diseases from the new settlers.

Ute leader Walkara spoke his native Ute language, as well as Spanish and English.

What happened when pioneers wanted to settle in American Indian regions? For a while, new settlers and Indians often got along well. Brigham Young advised settlers to feed the Indians rather than fight them. When food ran low during the winter, whites and Utes in Sanpete County worked together to haul food and supplies on sleds through the snow. Ute and Shoshone people also showed the new settlers how to dig for sego and thistle bulbs they could eat.

Whites and Indians also cooperated in other ways. After settlers moved into Sanpete County in 1850, measles broke out among the Ute Indians there. White settlers gave them medicines to help them get well. But cooperation usually did not last for long. Pretty quickly problems developed. Indians began to suffer. They suffered in two ways.

First, they began to lose their land. Their best hunting and gathering grounds were turned into townsites, grazing fields, and farmland. Indians often liked to camp near the streams and canyons where they could get water and kill animals for food. That was also the land pioneers wanted for their farmland. Deer and other animals fled into the high mountains, or were killed for food by the settlers.

The second way Indians suffered was from diseases. They caught diseases like smallpox and measles from white settlers. Thousands of the people died.

The pioneers also wanted to convert the American Indian people to Mormonism, and to teach them to be farmers. They wanted them to give up the Ute way, or the Goshute way, or the Navajo way. Most Indians did not want to give up their own ways. They wanted the new settlers to leave. But the settlers did not leave. They kept coming in larger and larger numbers.

Because they did not want new settlers living on their land, Indian people in Utah fought back. There were many small and large battles in Utah, plus three major wars. The Indians lost each of the wars.

The Walker War

The first war was the Walker War. It lasted for a year, from the summer of 1853 to the summer of 1854. The main leader was a Ute named Walkara. (White people called him "Walker.") He was born near the Spanish Fork River, a meeting ground for many bands of Utes. He was upset at the coming of new settlers. So he led his people in fighting back. There were many battles. The Utes were defeated. Walkara died of pneumonia the next year.

The Goshute War

The Goshutes' lifestyle had also been upset. Sheep and cattle were grazing over their land. Food was harder to find. They wanted to keep new settlers off their lands. So they attacked stage coaches and stations all along the route through Utah to California. After the United States Army was sent to Utah to fight them, they gave in.

The Black Hawk War

The Black Hawk War was long and costly. It was named after a Ute leader, Black Hawk, but Utes, Navajos, and Southern Paiutes all fought in it. They were all angered by the spreading of white settlements. They attacked Mormon towns mainly in Sanpete County and Sevier County, but also farther south. The Indians forced the new settlers to abandon twenty-five of their towns. Finally a peace treaty was signed.

Black Hawk died in 1870, two years after the Black Hawk War ended. He was buried in the mountains near Spring Lake in Utah County, just a few miles from his birthplace.

The Bear River Massacre

The biggest single battle between whites and Indians was the Bear River Massacre in Cache Valley. The U.S. Army killed more than three hundred Shoshone men, women, and children; destroyed their village, including about seventy tepees; and captured nearly two hundred of their horses.

Years after Black Hawk's death, miners dug up his remains. They ended up at the Mormon church's historical department. Now Black Hawk's remains have been given back to the Ute Tribe. His people have buried them at a place of honor.

Indian Reservations

After the Black Hawk War, the U.S. government forced most of the American Indian people in Utah to move to **reservations**. Those were areas set aside for Indians to live on. In all, seven reservations were established in Utah, and many more were made in other states. Look at the map of Utah's reservations on page 124.

Life on the reservations was hard. Most often the land was not as good as the land where the people had lived before. It was hard for a family to produce enough food to support itself.

There were rules, too. The people were not allowed to sing or dance. They could not perform their religious rituals and ceremonies. The United States government wanted them to give up their Indian culture. Even so, the people fought hard to keep their **traditions** and languages.

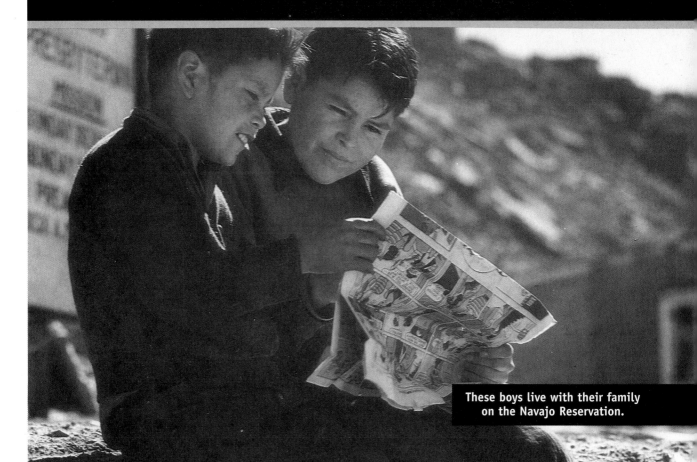

These boys live with their family on the Navajo Reservation.

Native Americans Today

Utah Indians were ignored and left alone on the reservations until the 1920s. They were very poor. They were given no schools. They were not allowed to make much money. Finally things began to change. In 1934 Indians won the right to have tribal councils and make their own laws and govern themselves. In 1946 they were paid millions of dollars for lands that had been taken from their ancestors. This money was divided among all the people, with each person getting a small share.

Today each tribe runs its own schools and businesses. For example, the Navajo Tribal Council decides what is best for the Navajos. The Ute Business Committee runs timber, irrigation, and ranch projects on Ute lands.

About half of Utah's Native Americans live along the Wasatch Front. Others live in towns around the state. Many Native Americans, however, still live on reservations. The Navajo Reservation has the most people. Utes who live on the Uintah-Ouray Reservation are the second largest group. A map of Utah reservations is on page 124.

Native Americans are important to Utah today. Some are teachers and principals, like Roy Talk, Gloria Thompson, and Jason Cuch. Forrest Cuch and Mark Maryboy work in government jobs. They are making things better for Indian people. Indians are doctors and lawyers. They are businesswomen and men, like Cal Nez. They are carpenters, like Katchee Mitchell, and also truck drivers. They are ranchers and farmers. Sometimes they wear traditional dress. Mostly they dress like anyone else who does the jobs they do. They share their arts, culture, songs, and talents with all of us.

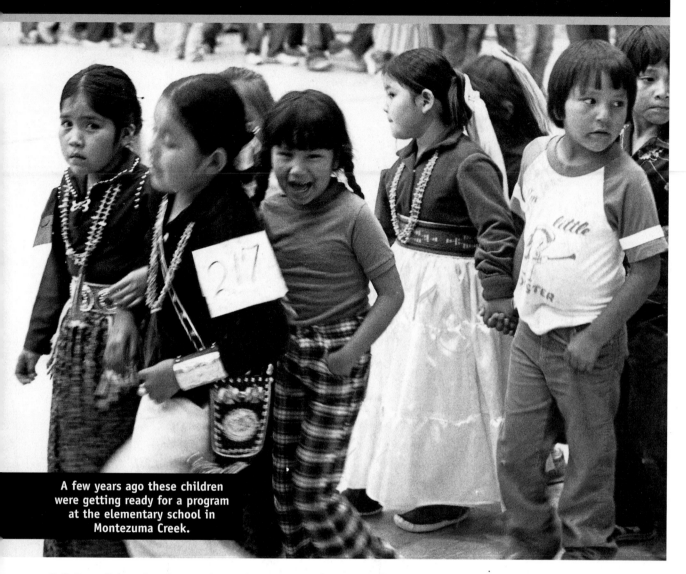

A few years ago these children were getting ready for a program at the elementary school in Montezuma Creek.

Gail Russell is a Southern Paiute. She grew up on a reservation in Arizona. In high school she studied business. That helped her to get jobs as a secretary. She is also concerned about Native American civil rights. Once she and her husband even marched to Washington, D.C., with thousands of other Native Americans. Their group moved inside of the Bureau of Indian Affairs to make a point about broken treaties. Another time, she and her husband and children traveled to Wounded Knee, South Dakota, to join a protest with the American Indian Movement (AIM). She had to quit her job as a secretary in the History Department at the University of Utah to do this.

Today, Gail Russell runs the Indian Walk-In Center in Salt Lake City, to help other Indians. The center gives food and clothing to people who need them. It gives advice to people. It sponsors powwows and teaches classes on tribal ceremonies.

Urshel Taylor is a Pima and Ute Indian. He grew up in Roosevelt, Utah, and graduated from Altamont High School in Duchesne County. Now he lives in Brigham City. He is an artist and sculptor. He carves figures of traditional Indian dancers out of wood. His sculptures are in galleries all over the western United States.

Utah Indian Reservations

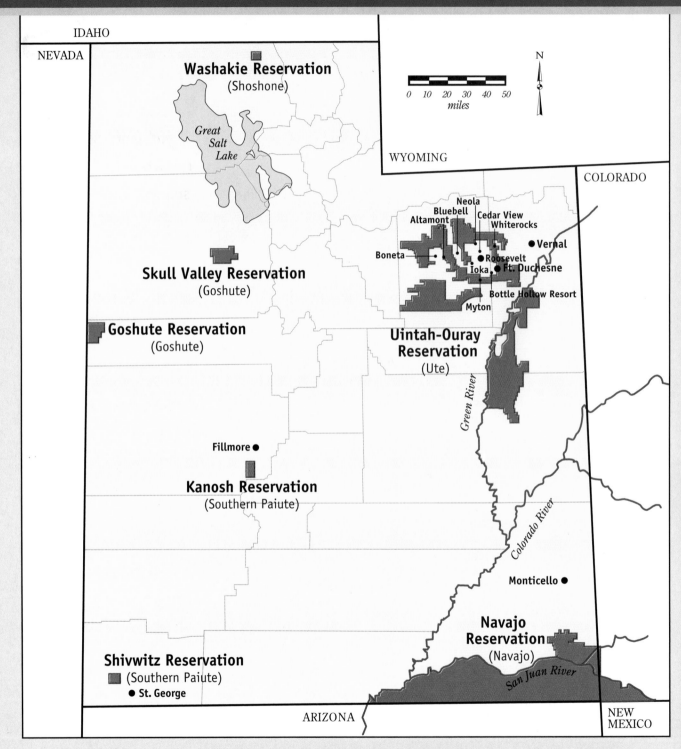

IDAHO

NEVADA

Washakie Reservation
(Shoshone)

Great Salt Lake

N

0 10 20 30 40 50
miles

WYOMING

COLORADO

Neola
Bluebell
Altamont   Cedar View
                Whiterocks
Boneta   ● Vernal
            ● Roosevelt
        Ioka ● Ft. Duchesne

Skull Valley Reservation
(Goshute)

Bottle Hollow Resort

Myton

Goshute Reservation
(Goshute)

**Uintah-Ouray
Reservation**
(Ute)

Green River

Fillmore ●

Kanosh Reservation
(Southern Paiute)

Colorado River

Monticello ●

**Navajo
Reservation**
(Navajo)

Shivwitz Reservation
■ (Southern Paiute)
● St. George

San Juan River

ARIZONA

NEW
MEXICO

Reservations were places the United States government set aside for different groups of American Indians.
Often the people were forced to move to the reservations. Now the people do not have to live on the reservations,
but many families still choose to live there. It is their home.

The Utah War

The story of white and American Indian relations is a sad part of Utah history. It is hard to hear about, but it is important. There is another story in early Utah history that is hard to hear about. That story deals with the Utah War. Here is what happened.

Government people in Washington, D.C. thought that the Mormons in Utah were **rebelling**, or going against, the United States. So, in the summer of 1857, the United States government sent an army to Utah. It was called Johnston's Army, because the commander was Colonel Johnston. The army was supposed to put down the rebellion.

However, the Mormon people were not really rebelling. They hoped that before there was any fighting, they could convince the government of that. But if the government did not believe them, they decided they would move out of Utah and find another place to live. They started to do that.

Everyone in the northern part of Utah, including people in Salt Lake City, left their homes and moved to the southern part. There they waited to see what the army would do. This was called the "move south." It took two months to complete. In all, 30,000 people joined the rush, packing their belongings, loading their wagons, and leaving their homes.

When Johnston's Army marched through Salt Lake City a year later, they found it almost **deserted**. Only a few people had stayed behind. The Utah people were going to set fire to the city if the soldiers decided to attack.

The Utah War ended when United States President Buchanan granted Mormons a "free and full pardon." Brigham Young then declared that "All who wish to return to their homes in Great Salt Lake City are at liberty to do so."

Soldiers stayed here for a long time, but they did not occupy any Utah towns. Instead, they established Camp Floyd, forty miles south of Salt Lake City.

The worst part of the Utah War was called the Mountain Meadows Massacre. Many people were killed. It happened soon after Mormons got word that Johnston's Army was on its way to Utah.

A wagon train of more than one hundred people were traveling through Utah on their way to California. Because the Mormons had already suffered persecution in many states, and because they knew the army was marching here, they were not feeling very good about the non-Mormons.

One soldier wrote that marching through Salt Lake was a strange sight. "Every man, woman, and child had ... departed—fled! It was substantially a city of the dead, and might have been depopulated by pest or famine."

Colonel Johnston brought soldiers to Utah. They thought the people here were against the United States government, which was not true. No shots were fired at the Mormons or the soldiers during the whole "Utah War." After a while, the soldiers actually helped the people by buying food and supplies from them.

The people in the wagon train did not like Mormons very much either. Some bragged that they had helped kill the Mormon leaders in Illinois.

In early September 1857, the members of the wagon train camped in the mountains of southern Utah near St. George. The place was called Mountain Meadows. A rider was sent to Salt Lake City to ask Brigham Young what to do. He said to let the people go without harming them. Before the rider could return to Southern Utah, a group of Mormons and Indians attacked them. The attackers killed everyone in the wagon train except seventeen children. It was a very sad time in the history of Utah.

Fort Douglas was built by the United States government. This is a picture of the horse stables in 1868. The fort is near where the University of Utah is now.

What Do You Think?

People have to live together and get along. They need to respect each other.
If they do not, terrible things can happen.

1. What makes it easy for you to get along with someone else? What makes it hard?

2. Have you ever had a difficult time being around someone, and then later you became friends? What changed?

3. If you have had to move to a new place, what things were exciting and good, and what things were hard for you?

Can You Remember?

1. Why did people come to Utah?

2. Why did pioneers start new towns?

3. What were some of the earliest settlements outside Salt Lake City?

4. Why did settlers and the American Indians disagree about settlement on lands the Indians lived on?

5. What started the Utah War?

Geography Tie-In

1. On a map of the world, find the countries most of the new immigrants came from. Name the continent they came from.

2. Trace with your finger on the map the route the immigrants probably took to get to Utah.

3. Write down all the different kinds of transportation they used to move here. (Don't forget walking!)

4. Find the town of St. George on the map. Do some research to see how the climate of St. George is different from the climate in the northern part of the state.

Words to Know

desert
rebel
reservation
self-sufficient
tradition

Most people in early Utah grew their own food and raised animals.

Life in Early Utah

Historians study the way people lived in the past. One important thing they study is ordinary people and their everyday lives. In this chapter we are going to discuss what life was like for ordinary people in early Utah after Salt Lake City was started.

Fitting In

In early Utah, most people lived in small, quiet, **rural** towns or on farms. Later, a few of the towns, like Salt Lake City and St. George, grew into cities.

Most of the people living in those towns were Mormons. A boy or girl could grow up and hardly ever meet someone who was not a Mormon. Mormons did not know much about other people or have much to do with them. People who were not Mormons seemed strange to them.

At first, it was hard for other people who came to Utah to fit in. An historian named Dale Morgan said that early Utah was a place that was very comfortable if you were a Mormon. It was very difficult if you were not.

People in Utah had to learn to understand other people and not **stereotype** them. Do you know what stereotype means? It means thinking you know what a person is like, just because that person belongs to a certain group. We should not stereotype people with disabilities, people of other races or religions, or people who have a lot more or less money than we do. It is important not to make a decision about what someone is like before you get to know them.

Early Towns and Early Homes

The towns in the early days looked pretty much the same throughout Utah. They had wide streets with ditches of water running on both sides. The water was for use in the house as well as for irrigation. Tall, thin poplar trees stood in rows. The towns looked like squares or rectangles, with streets running north and south, east and west. The church and other public buildings were located in a central square. At first houses were built of logs, and later of adobe or stone.

Log homes often had dirt roofs, wooden floors, and no windows. When the people could afford it, they had glass shipped from the East.

Look carefully at this photograph of a log cabin.
How many trees would you have to cut down to build it?
How many rooms do you think it has?
What keeps wind and snow from blowing in?
How are the corners hooked so it does not fall down?
Why do you suppose log houses were usually so small?
Notice the roof. It is made of wood boards with dirt on the top.

Here is part of a diary about what it was like to live in a house with a dirt roof:

*In the beginning of March we had a severe storm of rain and sleet, completely **saturating** the roofs, so that it rained as fast in the house as it did outside. . . . We had an oilcloth table-cover which we tacked over our heads where we ate, emptying the water into buckets every little while. Wraps and umbrellas were used while doing our cooking and housework. The storm lasted ten days. . . . It rained on us in the house for some time after it **abated** outside.* —Mary Isabella Horne

This drawing shows the inside of a log cabin.
What do you think it would be like to live in it?
Does it seem large or small?
Can you tell what was used for heat and light?

The inside of a cabin was often dark, especially if there was only one window. There was always a fireplace for heat. Later some cabins had stoves for heating and cooking. It was also used for cooking. Furniture was mostly homemade. Most people built a better house as soon as they could.

An adobe house took a long time to build, because the people had to make the bricks. But the house was often much larger than a cabin.

Look at the adobe house in this photograph. Adobe is a mixture of water, dirt, and straw. It is shaped into bricks and dried in the sun. Can you see the lines of bricks? People were lucky to have windows in their early houses. Before they had glass, they used greased paper or cloth to cover window openings.

Work, Work, Work

People had a lot to do, and they worked hard. About half the people were farmers. The rest did other things.

Each village needed:

- Sawmills to cut boards from logs.
- Gristmills to grind wheat and corn into flour.
- Tanneries to make leather boots and shoes for people, and harnesses for horses and mules.
- Blacksmith shops to make metal shoes for horses and oxen, and iron tires for wagon wheels. They also made metal tools, guns, and nails.
- Carpenters to build buildings.
- Bricklayers to build walls and buildings.

These were only some of the jobs that were necessary. Can you think of other jobs that would be important?

Men and women and children worked together. Women did more than work in the house and take care of the children. They also worked on the farm and in the fields. Both men and women worked in the fields planting and harvesting the crops, milking the cows, feeding and watering the animals, and cleaning the stables and barnyard.

In the summer, settlers often baked bread in an outdoor oven so the house wouldn't get so hot indoors.

Women used scraps of cloth to make quilts. They used good pieces of worn-out clothes, too. The patterns were handed down from mothers to their daughters. Children often played underneath the quilting frames as the women sewed the tiny stitches.

Christinia Oleson Warnick kept a diary about her life in the town of Deseret. Here is some of what she did:

- Helped build the house, fireplace, and chimney.
- Plowed, planted, and fertilized the land.
- Helped dig irrigation ditches.
- Cut and stacked wild hay from the river bottoms, for the cows.
- Sheared the sheep.
- Made clothes.
- Walked from town to town selling butter and eggs.

Food for All

People ate mostly meat, wheat, milk and cheese, corn, potatoes, and other vegetables.

The people grew most of their own food in gardens and orchards. During the summer and fall there was more food because in those months people had gardens. They could eat fresh peas, beans, squash, cabbage, cauliflower, lettuce, dandelion greens, and beets. They had trees and bushes that produced apricots, cherries, plums, peaches, currants, gooseberries, and raspberries.

Farming was hard work. This is the family farm behind the Lion House in Salt Lake City, which was one of Brigham Young's homes.

(Painting by Weggeland)

The women dried some fruits and vegetables and made them into jam. Cool, underground pits or cellars kept vegetables as fresh as possible.

Fresh milk from cows and goats was kept in cellars or other cool places. Cream skimmed from the top of the milk was used in cooking, or to make butter.

Many families had a flock of chickens, geese and ducks. They were used as food, and their feathers were used to stuff pillows and mattresses.

Winter was a time for killing cattle and hogs. The cold weather helped to keep the meat fresh. A quarter of beef could be wrapped in cloth and hung on the north side of the house, where it was cooler. Pork was turned into smoked hams, sausage, and headcheese.

Making Clothes

When people's clothes wore out or got too small, they couldn't just go to the store and buy new ones. They had to make their own. The women made most of the clothing for themselves and everyone else. That was one of their main jobs. Sometimes they could buy cloth brought in from states in the East. Otherwise, they had to make their own cloth, too.

Mary Ann Orton lived in Parowan as a young girl. She wrote in her diary: "My mother herded sheep, sheared them, washed and carded the wool; then spun it and wove it into cloth. From it she made blankets, shawls, and clothing."

Pioneers raised sheep, sheared the sheep, then used the wool to make yarn. Then they used a spinning wheel to twist the wool fibers into yarn. To make candles, they dipped string into a vat of melted wax over and over again until the candle was fat enough.

Making the Things They Needed

Besides clothing, people in early Utah also had to make many other things they needed. They made soap, candles, brooms, wooden bottles, spoons, cups, plates, chairs, tables, beds, and tools.

Soap-making in the spring was a full day's work. Soap was made from wood ashes and animal grease. It took many bushels of ashes and many pounds of grease to make a barrel of soap. But that much soap lasted a long time.

People had to be very careful and not waste anything. They had to get as much use from things as they possibly could. Children grew up having their mothers tell them, "Use it up, wear it out, make it do, or do without."

This is a candle mold used over 150 years ago.

Church Influence

The Mormon church was still very important in people's lives.

- It provided jobs for people on public works projects. If a carpenter, or painter, or stonecutter, or anyone else could not find a job, the church leaders provided one. The idea was that the community as a whole should look out for everyone.
- It sometimes asked people to start certain businesses that the people in a town needed. It might ask them to start making iron, or grow silkworms to make silk.
- It sometimes told people how much money they would be paid for their jobs.
- It sometimes told businesses how much they could charge for the things they sold.

Brigham Young wanted the people to raise silkworms so they could make silk cloth. He had mulberry trees and silkworms brought from France. A lady from Northern Italy, Susanna Cardon, gave instructions in spinning and making silk.

> "My brothers and I had only one spelling book and one slate for the three of us. We had no copy books or notebooks. Quill pens were used to write with and pieces of lead were used for pencils. The windows were covered with white cloth to let in the light and we had benches to sit on."
>
> —*A young girl writing about her first school in the Salt Lake Valley.*

Mary Jane Dilworth started a school in her tent in the Old Fort soon after the pioneers arrived.

Schools

Schools began almost as soon as the pioneers came to Utah. In October 1847, just three months after they arrived, a seventeen-year-old girl started a school in her tent in the Old Fort. Her name was Mary Jane Dilworth. There were six students to begin with. Rough logs were used for seats, and Miss Dilworth's desk was an old camp stool. Her younger sister, Marie, was one of the students. Here is what she remembered:

I attended the first school in Utah, taught by my sister Mary Jane. . . . I remember Mary Jane saying to us: "Come, children, come. We will begin now." We entered the tent, sat down on the logs in a circle, and one of the "brethren" offered a prayer. There were nine of us that first day. We learned one of the psalms of the Bible, and sang songs.

Instead of pencils and paper, the children used charcoal and wrote on smooth logs or bark from white birch trees. They also mixed clay with water to make a kind of ink.

After this first school began, more and more schools were started. Marie Nebeker went to an early school. This is what she wrote about it:

The little school I attended was in a log cabin. The room was very uncomfortable and very cold in winter. Pegs were thrust into the logs around the room, and on these were rough boards for seats. The smaller children sat on blocks, which they brought from home. The teacher sat at one end of the room, and watched the boys and girls. She was never angry at us, but always patient and kind. There were no blackboards or maps.

School began at 9 o'clock. We sang songs and then the teacher always prayed. We had "mental" exercise in arithmetic, and then the teacher read to us from the geography. We girls sewed every day in school. The boys were organized into groups and marched off to the fields to gather sagebrush for the little stove that was in the center of the room.

Friday afternoon was looked forward to with pleasure, for if we had been good during the week we had a "spelling match." There were also "geography matches" and arithmetic problems to solve. We often danced in the schoolroom, and one of the happy events was the closing programme at the end of the winter or at Christmas time.

Early schools had all the grades in one room. How is this school different from your classroom?
(Painting by Dolly S. Rockwood)

This photo of a school in Cove Fort shows the different ages of the students, what their clothes looked like, and what their school looked like.

"Bring every book, map, chart or diagram that may contain interesting, useful, and attractive matter, to gain the attention of children and cause them to love to learn to read."

—*Brigham Young, 1847*

The early Mormon pioneers also started a university. They called it the University of Deseret. Later it became the University of Utah. At first only men took classes. In a few years, ninety-nine men and eighty-eight women attended.

Education for everybody was important. Brigham Young said:

> *Women are useful not only to sweep houses, wash dishes, make beds, and raise babies. They should stand behind the counter, study laws of physics, or become good book-keepers and be able to do the business in any county house, and all this to enlarge their sphere of usefulness for the benefit of society at large.*

Time for Fun

Life for the early pioneers was different in many ways from life today. There was a lot of hard work to do. But people found time for fun.

Bring on the band! Pioneers had instruments coming across the plains. Each town also usually had a band.

There were no radios, TVs, movies, or video games. So how did people spend their time when they were not working? Music, drama, and dance were important. Every town had a choir and a band. Sometimes they had several bands—a brass band and a string band. People put on plays, too. Almost every town had an acting company, and they held dances all the time. Men, women, and children loved to dance.

The first Christmas in Utah, 1847, was celebrated in a home with a lively dance.

To pay to get into a dance, a young man "paid in kind." This meant that he could pay with a piece of meat, eggs, or even an animal skin. Squash, lettuce, potatoes, and other vegetables were taken at the door.

A traveler named Richard Burton visited Salt Lake City in 1862. He wrote a book about what he saw. Everyone danced, he said. "The Prophet dances, the Apostles dance, the Bishops dance."

Dancing parties were held often and went late into the night. There was usually a fiddle player, and maybe someone playing an accordion, or even an organ. Round and round in different patterns men and women, boys and girls marched. Often a woman had to leave the floor because her baby was crying. No mother remained at home on account of the children. Everyone came along.

Most holidays ended with a grand ball. It began with dinner, then dancing until 2:00 or 3:00 in the morning, and finally more eating as people finished the leftover food almost in time for breakfast.

People danced whenever they got a chance. Sometimes they danced during their lunch hour. Sometimes they danced after work. When a county courthouse was built in Brigham City in 1856, Sarah Squires remembered that "Among the first things done was the construction of a large platform, where the workmen might dance a quadrille [square dance] or two before returning to their afternoon work; or where, after the day's work they might go for a few hours of amusement."

In some towns dancing schools were established. Both children and adults went. The first one in Brigham City was under the direction of John Bynon. He taught dances with

On holidays the people had horse racing, ball games, foot races, and contests of strength.

names like "Money Musk" and "Twin Sisters." A man named Blindman Jones furnished the music with his fiddle.

When children got tired of dancing, they played games outdoors. One of their favorites was Sheep Over the River. First they built a big fire. One person was chosen to be the wolf. All the rest were sheep. The sheep ran and hid. The wolf stayed by the fire and then called, "Wolf over the river." The sheep replied, "What will you have?" Wolf: "A good, fat sheep." Sheep: "Catch us if you can." And off ran the wolf in search of the sheep until they all were found.

Another favorite game was Pull the Rope. A rope was laid over a river or stream. Teams of children tugged on each end of the rope and tried to pull the other team into the river. Games called Steal-Sticks and Duck-Stones were also popular. Not many people remember those games today.

Polygamy

Family life in Utah was different, and also very interesting. The reason was polygamy. Polygamy means that husbands have more than one wife at a time. Mormons also called it "plural marriage."

In Utah most married men had only one wife, just like men in the rest of the country. But many men in Utah had two or three wives, or even more. Brigham Young had more than fifty wives and more than fifty children. But even in families where the men had only one wife, just about everybody in the Mormon church defended polygamy.

Sometimes the husband and all of his wives and children lived together in the same house. Sometimes each wife and her children had a separate house. Then the husband took turns staying with each family.

Annie Clark Tanner grew up in Farmington. Her father had two wives. One wife had ten children. The other had eleven. They lived in separate houses across the street from each other. "As a child, I went freely from one home to the other," she said. "A cordial family companionship existed between the children of the two homes." She called her father's other wife "Aunt Mary."

Brigham Young built the Lion House in Salt Lake City for many of his wives and children. A large lion carved out of stone was above the front door. The basement had a long dining room where up to seventy people could eat together. The first floor had bedrooms for nine wives. The top floor had twenty bedrooms for children. Some of his other wives

Alice Young was a daughter of Brigham and Mary Ann Young. She grew up in a polygamous family.

The Lion House is in Salt Lake City, a block away from Temple Square. It was one of Brigham Young's houses for some of his wives and children. You can visit the Lion House and the Beehive House next door and see the children's bedrooms, their schoolroom, and the family store in the back room.

and children had separate houses in Salt Lake City. Some of them lived in other cities in Utah.

Sometimes plural marriages were difficult for the husband and the wives. Other times everyone got along well. Plural wives living in the same house often shared the work. One wife might make clothes for everyone. Another wife would do all the cooking. Another wife did the ironing. The wives often did some chores together, like washing clothes. They nursed each other in ill health. They usually did not all go out to church or a party together. They took turns staying home and taking care of all the children.

Here is what one person remembered about growing up in a plural family:

In 1859 father married "Aunt Willie," his first wife. Eight years later, with her consent, he married "Aunt Joe" and took her to share the home with him and his first wife. In 1877 "Aunt Rhoda," the third wife, was brought to this home. She was welcomed by the other wives and introduced

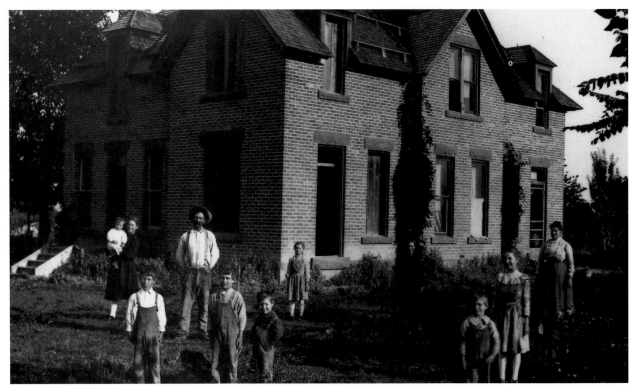

This large house was home to a family who lived in polygamy. The children always had a mother and several "aunts" at home, as well as many other children to play with.

to the children as another mother who had come to live with them.

By 1880 the family had increased in numbers until it was necessary to have more room, so father bought another place and "Aunt Joe" and "Aunt Rhoda" were moved into the new home. Here they lived, until again the family needed larger quarters. Then the third home was provided.

Each did the part of the work she liked best to do. "Aunt Joe" always milked the cow and did other outside work, while "Aunt Rhoda" did the dish washing and other housework. Washing, ironing and sewing they did together. The older children helped whichever mother needed them. The children went from one home to the other freely and were always welcomed by the mother.

When people who were not Mormons came to Utah, they did not like polygamy. They were shocked and angered. After a while, the United States government passed laws making polygamy illegal. But Mormons said that God wanted them to live that way. There was not just one way of arranging families. They thought polygamy was a better marriage system than the typical family. Polygamy caused many problems for the Mormons and other people living in Utah. We will discuss the problems in Chapter 10.

What Do You Think?

Talk with your friends about these things.

1. Explore ways that people who have different ideas can get along, and learn from each other.

2. Ask your teacher to tell you about people in history who have been brave and stood up for what they believed in, even if they didn't think the same as everyone else.

3. Compare the lifestyle of the children in early Utah to your life now. Make a list of things you like better about each time period. Include homes, food, work, clothes, and things you do for fun.

Can You Remember?

1. Most early Mormon towns were laid out alike. Name three features they had alike.

2. Who started Utah's first school?

3. What was hard about life in early Utah?

4. What kinds of entertainment did early Utahns enjoy?

5. What is adobe? How was it used?

6. What are three things pioneers had to make themselves?

Geography Tie-In

1. Do you live in a rural or urban place? A rural town is out in the country, with farms. An urban town is a much larger city, with many stores, businesses, schools, and homes closer together. You might live in a combination of both.

2. If you were an early settler and had to grow all of your own food, what kind of land would you look for? What kinds of things from nature would you need?

Words to Know

abate

rural

saturate

stereotype

The remains of a pony express station can still be seen in the west desert of Utah.

Change Comes to Utah

When the pioneers first came to Utah, the Salt Lake Valley was very isolated. It was a thousand miles from other white settlements. It took people three months to get here. That is one reason the Mormons came in the first place.

But soon things changed. As methods of **communication** and **transportation** got better and better, Utah people became connected with the rest of the country by wagon trains, stagecoaches, the pony express, the telegraph, and the railroads. The completion of the **transcontinental** railroad was the most important of all.

Stagecoaches brought the mail and passengers. It took a lot of skill to drive a stagecoach. Strong horses, bad weather, and terrible dirt roads made the job hard.

Wagon Trains and Stagecoaches

Early pioneers wanted to be self-sufficient, but they soon found that was impossible. They could not make enough of everything they needed. They had to buy things from outside of Utah. Soon wagon trains brought loads of supplies here. They brought sugar, soap, hats, shoes, nails, bullets, and just about everything else people needed. In pioneer days there were hundreds of wagons on the roads, loaded with things people needed.

Wagon trains also carried mail. Mostly, though, the mail came on stagecoaches. So did passengers. Stagecoaches were much faster than wagon trains. The coaches took about fourteen days to travel from the Mississippi River to Utah. Utahns looked forward to stagecoaches from the East that might bring letters from family and friends.

The Pony Express

The pony express was a mail delivery service. Young men on horseback carried letters from Missouri to California as fast as they could ride. There were several pony express stations in Utah.

Here are some facts about the pony express:
1. It operated from April 1860 to October 1861.
2. There were 190 relay stations.
3. Riders went 1,966 miles from Missouri to Sacramento, California.
4. It used 400 horses.
5. The horses galloped about 9 miles an hour.
6. It employed 80 riders, usually boys 18 years old.
7. It charged $3 to carry a letter.
8. It went broke after the telegraph wires were connected. Then messages could be sent from coast to coast on the telegraph.

Pony express riders rode fast and hard.

Painting by William Jackson ◀

Activity
Interpreting Facts about the Pony Express

1. How long did it take a letter to get from Missouri to California?
2. If the stations were evenly spaced, how far apart were they?
3. Suppose the riders traveled one hundred miles before they rested. They could stop only two minutes at each stop. Then how long did it take them to travel one hundred miles?
4. Why were there more horses than men?
5. How many months did the pony express last?
6. Why did it go out of business?

Painting by Gregory Sievers ▼

The Railroad

After the pioneers came, the event that changed Utah the most was the railroad.

The United States Congress voted to build a railroad that would go all the way across the country. It would be called the transcontinental railroad. Two companies were organized to build it. One started in Omaha, Nebraska, and worked west. The other started in Sacramento, California, and went east.

It took an army of workers to lay all those miles of track. Most of the workers were immigrants. Often they did not speak English. The largest number were from Ireland and China. Immigrants have always made important contributions to this country. One of the biggest was the building of the transcontinental railroad.

The men in each company worked hard to lay as much track as they could. The work was difficult and often dangerous. Much of the track was laid on flat prairie land, but some of it had to go through the Sierra Nevadas and the Rocky Mountains. The hot deserts were a problem, and the cold winters in the mountains were terrible for the workers. Many died while working on the track.

Trains changed the lives of the people in a big way. Now people, animals, and goods could go from place to place much faster than by wagons.

Men from China are carrying coal to the trains. The coal was burned to heat water, which made steam. Steam power made the trains move.

At first some American workers doubted that the small Chinese were strong enough for the job. But the Chinese turned out to be very hard workers indeed. One of the railroad owners said, "If we found we were in a hurry for a job, it was better to put the Chinese on at once."

The Golden Spike

"Hail to the Highway of Nations; Utah Bids You welcome!" These were the words on banners announcing the joining of the railroads.

In 1869 the two rail lines met at Promontory, Utah. Thousands of Utahns were there to watch. Puffing steam, two railroad engines faced each other on the tracks.

The governor of California took a swing with the hammer at the last railroad spike, made of gold. He missed. He swung again, and missed again. Finally a railroad worker took over. He had driven many railroad spikes, and he didn't miss. With one swing he drove the golden spike in.

The news was sent by telegraph across the nation. There were cheers, bands, and banners.

This is the most famous photograph of the joining of the rails at Promontory, Utah.

Transcontinental Railroad

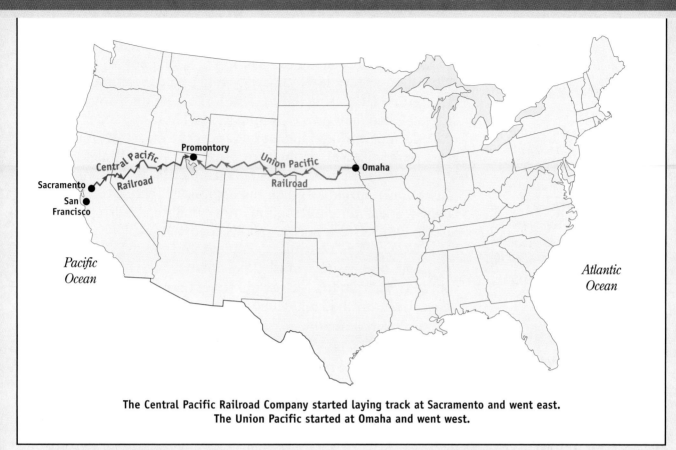

The Central Pacific Railroad Company started laying track at Sacramento and went east.
The Union Pacific started at Omaha and went west.

A Salt Lake City resident, Leo Oliver, remembers his father's job:

*My parents came here in 1885 to work on the railroad. My father was a Pullman **porter**. He'd take care of the sleeping department. Back then, if you got on the train and went to Los Angeles or Frisco, he'd make the bed for you. They called them sleepers. My father made $27.50 a month. He worked all day and half the night for $27.50 a month.*

More Railroad Lines

Soon more railroad lines were built throughout Utah. First a railroad line was built from Promontory to Salt Lake City. A train station was built in Salt Lake. Soon people could go almost anywhere in Utah by traveling on the railroad.

Some cities—including Salt Lake, Ogden, Provo, and Logan—had their own railway systems. These city trains were called street railways. In Salt Lake City the first street railway cars were pulled along their tracks by horses and mules.

After the railroad came to Utah, many black men worked for it. The railroad was their most important employer. Some men worked on construction crews building and repairing track. Others were porters, cooks, and waiters.

Now it was possible to travel from coast to coast by railroad, and the trip would take only six days. People could get to Utah from the Mississippi River in only one and a half days. Before, it had taken about one hundred days to go that far by covered wagon.

The railroad made it easier for people to buy from other cities in the country, and sell their things. Utahns began sending large amounts of wheat and fruits to people in other parts of the country.

The Union Pacific Railroad hired mostly blacks to work on the trains.

Mining Boom!

The railroad made another big difference in Utah. In fact, the railroad caused a mining boom.

Utah was rich in **minerals** such as salt and coal. Long before the railroad came, people had also found a lot of **ore** with precious metals in Utah. Early settlers mined gold, silver, copper, zinc, and lead.They didn't mine to make money selling to others. They mined just enough to get coal for their stoves, or iron to make tools, or lead to make bullets. But mining did not become important until after the railroad came. Until then, there was no way to ship large amounts of minerals to buyers outside of Utah.

Soon after the railroad came the two most common ways to make a living in early Utah were farming and mining. The town of Murray is a good example of a town that started as a farming town and then changed. At first, most people there supported themselves and their families by farming. Soon mining became more and more important. By the early 1900s, more than half the people worked in nearby copper mines or in smelters. In the smelters the minerals were taken out of the rock and turned into metal.

Railroad cars hauled the coal and ore from the mines to the smelters to places far away. Look at the workers. Do you see some boys? How old do you think they are? Families who needed money often took their sons out of school and got them jobs in the mines.

Children in the Mines

Often young children worked in mines. In fact they worked in all kinds of other jobs. If mothers and fathers were not paid enough to support their families, their children had to help out. Most children left school at least by the age of fourteen, often earlier, and went to work full time. That meant ten or twelve hours a day, six days a week. Life in early Utah was a steady round of work.

Immigrant Workers

Immigrants came to work in the mines, just as they had come to work on the railroad. Many of them did not speak English. Most were young, single men, although many miners brought their families.

Danger

Miners were paid only about $3 a day. They worked ten or twelve hours a day. Working in mines far under the ground was dangerous. People might fall from the mine elevators, called hoists, that went deep into the ground. Or the hoists might break. Miners might be hit by falling rocks or get run over by ore cars. An alarming number of miners also got lung diseases from breathing so much dust.

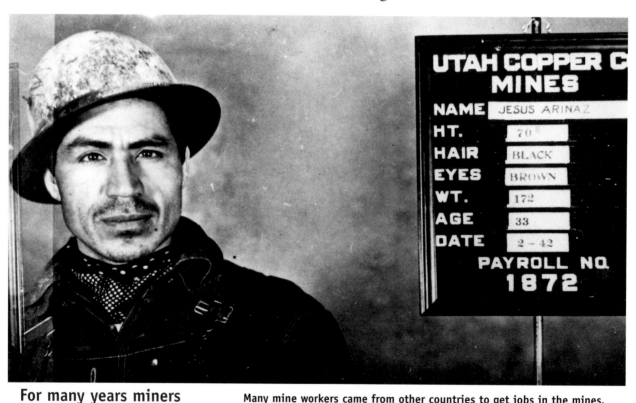

For many years miners were all men. Today women also work in mines. It was a long time before people thought it was all right for women to work in mines.

Many mine workers came from other countries to get jobs in the mines. What can you learn about this man from the sign?

Besides dust, the air in mines could be filled with deadly gas. That is why miners took a canary down into the mines with them. If the bird stayed alive, they knew the air was good. But if the canary died, they knew the air was poisonous, and they got out quickly. Gases in mines caused explosions, and mines also caved in.

Utah Mining Towns, 1800s

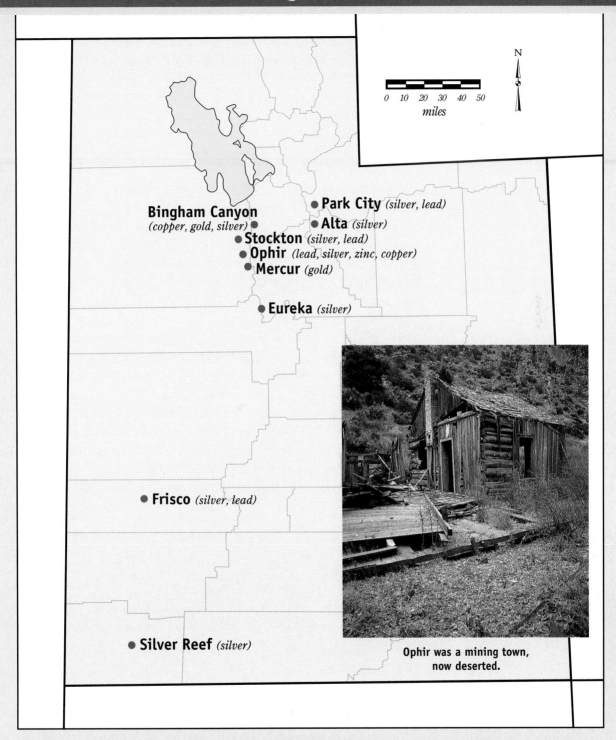

N

0 10 20 30 40 50
miles

Park City *(silver, lead)*

Bingham Canyon
(copper, gold, silver)

Alta *(silver)*

Stockton *(silver, lead)*

Ophir *(lead, silver, zinc, copper)*

Mercur *(gold)*

Eureka *(silver)*

Frisco *(silver, lead)*

Silver Reef *(silver)*

Ophir was a mining town,
now deserted.

This map shows some of the most important mining towns and what was mined there.

Mining Boom

In 1860 only four people in Utah made their living as miners. Just ten years later, there were 500 miners. Twenty years later almost 10,000 people in Utah worked in the mines.

Instead of going to work on the farms, or in stores, more and more people went to work in mines deep underground. Mines and mining towns were all over Utah.

Mining Towns

With the development of mining, Utah had a new kind of town besides Mormon villages. Mining towns like Silver Reef, Alta, Park City, and Bingham were very different from Mormon villages. They were not built according to the City of Zion plan. For that matter, they were not built according to any plan. People did not work together to build the city. They just built their own houses the way they wanted to. Often the houses were unpainted wood. The streets were narrow and winding.

Some mining towns later became ski resorts, like Alta and Park City. Others became ghost towns.

Silver Reef is a ghost town in the mountains near Leeds, in Washington County. In 1875 people heard that silver had been found there. Almost two thousand miners and their families moved there in just a few months. When they first arrived, they did not want to spend much time planning a city or building houses. They wanted to get right to work in the mines. So they lived in tents or small shacks. Later they built better houses and other buildings.

Soon Silver Reef had a main street with a general store and a stable. There were also a blacksmith shop, a boarding house, a dance hall, and several saloons. Then a school was built, and the Catholic church opened a hospital. Food was hauled in by wagon from nearby towns and farms.

When the silver ran out, the mines closed and people moved away. It was not long before the busy boom town became a ghost town.

Alta, in the mountains by Salt Lake City, was once a mining town. It is now a ski resort.

Many People Come to Utah

The railroad and the mines brought more and more people to Utah. They came from many places in the world. Utah became a **mosaic** of cultures, religions, and skin shades.

If you were to suddenly find yourself in Utah one hundred years ago, you could tell that Utah was changing just by looking around.

There were new churches, temples, and synagogues, for many religions. In Salt Lake City, Italians and many Spanish-speaking people went to the Catholic Cathedral of the Madeleine and Our Lady of Guadalupe Catholic Mission. But some of them went to Mormon churches. Greeks ususally went to the Holy Trinity Greek Orthodox Church. Russians and Slavs and Poles went to the Congregation Montefiore Jewish Synagogue. Many Japanese and Chinese went to the Buddhist Temple.

The Japanese Church of Christ, the Trinity African Methodist Episcopal Church, the Emanual Baptist Church, the Presbyterian Church, and many others were in Salt Lake City. Other towns also had churches of many religions.

If you kept looking, you would see Greek weddings and Yugoslavian funerals. In the Salt Lake Cemetery there was a Japanese section, a Chinese section, a Jewish section, a Catholic section, and a section for Mormon church leaders.

You would hear many languages on the streets, because many newcomers did not speak English. They spoke the language they had learned growing up.

"I was so homesick when I came. . . . Two years after I married my husband in the Salt Lake Catholic Cathedral. We had a big dinner at my aunt and uncle's house. Roast lamb, . . . chicken, honey pastries. Dancing, music."

—*Sarah Attey, immigrant from Lebanon to Utah in 1907*

Many churches started their own schools. This is the Presbyterian Church and Parsonage School in Salt Lake City. It was built in 1874.

Catholic people came to Utah to build churches, schools, and hospitals. Catholic children attended a school outing to the Saltair Resort in 1904.

Newspapers in many languages were sold on the street corners in early Utah.

Albert "Speck" Williams was born a slave. He was a cowboy in Utah, and often said he knew all the outlaws in Butch Cassidy's group.

Martha Perkins Howell, Lucinda Flake Stevens, and Belle Oglesby were descendants of Green Flake, who came into the Salt Lake Valley with the advance party of Brigham Young.

African Americans

One group who came early in our history were blacks. African American is a more modern name for this group. They were here as fur trappers before the pioneers came. They were part of the Mormon's advance party. After that they continued to come.

A good example is Isaac and Jane Manning James and their children, Sylvester and Silas. They arrived in Salt Lake in the fall of 1847, just a few months after the advance party. They were free, not slaves. Jane Manning James became an outstanding person in Utah's early black community. She and her brother Isaac had lived and worked in the Nauvoo house of Joseph Smith. In Utah, the James family went into farming, and so did their children. When Jane died, the president of the Mormon church spoke at her funeral.

Many of Utah's early blacks lived in Salt Lake City, or in a part of the Salt Lake Valley called Union. The cemetery there has many of their graves. Blacks also lived in

Detective Paul Howell was the first black policeman in Utah.

other parts of Utah. Frederick Sion came to Utah in 1862 with his wife Ellen and daughter Eliza. They settled near Logan, where he worked as one of the town's shoemakers.

The United States Civil War was fought mostly in the southern part of the country. One issue of the war was slavery. When it ended, slavery was against the law everywhere in the United States. Some former slaves left Utah to go back to their homes in the South. Some stayed here.

Some men came to Utah in the late 1800s as soldiers. They belonged to all-black cavalry units. American Indians called them "buffalo soldiers" because their hair reminded the Indians of the shaggy mane of the buffalo. They built Fort Duchesne in the Uintah Basin. They guarded stage and railway lines, and opened and cleared roads.

Because of discrimination, the black people were often left out of the social and cultural life of their towns. They developed their own groups. Families were very important to them. So was religion. Gospel music filled the air near the churches.

There were also black clubs, community centers, women's organizations, newspapers, and sports teams in Utah.

Hispanic Americans

Hispanic Americans are one of the largest groups in Utah today. They began coming to Utah about a hundred years ago from other states, like Colorado and New Mexico, and from the country of Mexico.

When they first came to Utah, they were farm workers. Then they began to work on the railroad. Many others came to work in the mines. Like other groups, they brought their culture with them.

One custom Mexican people brought to Utah had to do with Christmas morning. Children rose early to open their gifts. Then they visited neighbors to ask for sweets—*pedir las crismas*. When someone answered the door, the children chanted:

Oremos, Oremos	Let's pray, let's pray
angelitos semos	Little angels are we
del cielo venimos	Who have come from Heaven
a pedir algo venimos	to ask for charity.

This was to show how important it was to be kind to strangers who might indeed be angels from heaven asking for food or lodging.

Many Spanish-speaking children came to Utah with their parents. They had to learn a new language and American customs. Their parents were often given low-paying jobs because they could not speak English.

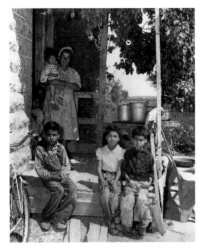

These children grew up near Ogden. There were twelve children in the family. Their parents had moved from Mexico in 1925 to do farm work. "Being a poor family was tough," said Franklin, the oldest son, "but the family stuck together." The family had a garden, chickens, and milk cows. All the children except the tiny ones had to work in the fields. After World War II both parents got jobs at Hill Air Force Base. "Life was better after that," said Josie, one of the daughters. They bought some land and built a two-bedroom house. The girls slept in one room and the boys slept in another. The children liked school.

Mexicans also brought their marriage customs to Utah. If a young man was interested in a girl, he first asked permission from her parents to take her on dates. If eventually he wanted to marry her, he asked his father to visit the girl's parents to ask for the marriage.

After the wedding ceremony, guests paraded to the house of the bride's parents. Along the way, a violinist and a guitarist played a simple wedding tune. There a fiesta was held. Guests were served a special dinner. After dinner, they held a wedding dance. When the dance was over, one of the musicians sang the wedding song, *entrega de novios*. It was a kind of blessing on the new couple. Then the new husband and wife knelt down before their parents and grandparents to receive a formal blessing.

Chinese Americans

The first Chinese people who came to Utah worked on the transcontinental railroad. After they finished it, some of them kept working for the railroad. Others quit, but stayed in Utah, some became vegetable farmers. Some opened restaurants, laundries, or other businesses in Utah cities.

Isabella Wilson remembered growing up in Ogden:

Pressing our noses flat against the windowpane, we saw the many colored Chinese lanterns made of paper, colored Chinese bowls, and we saw the Chinese eat with chopsticks, rice and chicken cooked together. Usually they knew us and were friendly. Many times they gave us Chinese candy or a Chinese handkerchief. They wore blue Chinese shoes or a type of sandal, blue trousers, trimmed in black, and a white sack coat.

One way to find out about what things were like in the past is to read old newspapers. Here is one story from the *Salt Lake Tribune* in 1897:

A prominent feature of nearly all New Year's parades was a huge Chinese dragon two hundred feet long which progressed along the street like a gigantic centipede. The dragon itself, which swayed from side to side, had a head six feet tall spitting fire from its red mouth.

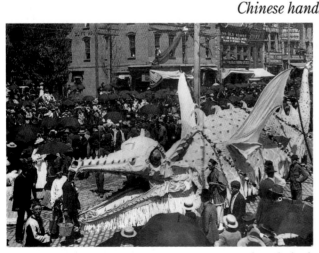

This Chinese dragon was part of Utah's 50-year statehood celebration parade.

Italian Americans

Like the Chinese, many Italians who came to Utah first worked on the railroads. Then they often started their own businesses.

Tony Scuimbato was born in Ruzzito, Italy. After he learned the family trade of shoemaking from his uncle, he came to the United States. He first went to New York City, but did not like it there. Eventually he found his way to Utah.

Soon after he got here, Tony Scuimbato met a young girl named Elizabeth Phillips. Even though he was twenty-four years old and she was only fourteen, they were soon married. He went to work in the mines in Bingham, but left after awhile to start his own shoe business in Midvale.

At first Mr. Scuimbato worked every day, twelve hours a day. People came from all over for him to make their shoes and boots and repair them. He and his wife had ten children. His son, Robert, said, "I can remember my father lining all ten of us up and going down the line checking shoes to see whose needed fixing."

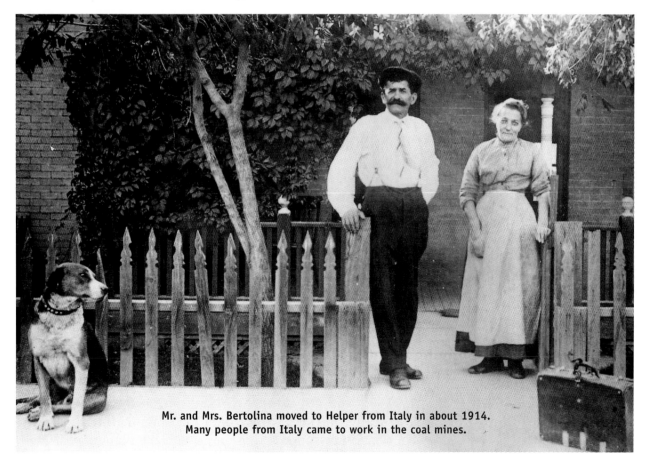

Mr. and Mrs. Bertolina moved to Helper from Italy in about 1914. Many people from Italy came to work in the coal mines.

Japanese New Year

When the Japanese in Utah celebrated their New Year, they thoroughly cleaned their houses. They took the last bath of the year to wash off the old year's dirt. People paid all of their debts. They exchanged greeting cards. They prepared food to be eaten during the first week of the new year.

The food included the golden Tai fish, baked whole with its eyes wide open. It was covered with shredded radishes. Eating it meant that all was well. They drank a Japanese rice wine called Saki.

Japanese Americans

The Japanese also first came to Utah mainly as railroad workers. Later many of them went into farming. Utah's celery and strawberry crops were known all over the United States in the early 1900s. They were produced mainly by Japanese farmers.

At first, mostly Japanese men came here alone to work. After a while, they wanted to get married. So women sent pictures of themselves to Utah. A man would look at the photographs and decide which woman he wanted to send for. When she arrived they would get married. The women were called "picture brides."

Edward "Daigoro" Hashimoto ran a business in Salt Lake City in the early 1900s.

After the women came to Utah, they often ran boarding houses. Often the husband's brothers, cousins, and other relatives lived with them. These women cooked large meals and filled an endless number of lunch buckets. They washed clothes by hand with homemade soap, and baked bread, sometimes in large, outdoor ovens. They grew vegetables and canned fruit.

Immigrant Neighborhoods

New neighborhoods were a visible sign that more different kinds of people were coming to Utah. Immigrants often lived together in neighborhoods with people from their own country. They did not scatter throughout a city. They opened restaurants and shops that sold food from their native lands. They read newspapers written in their own languages. They built their own businesses and churches.

Greektown

One **ethnic** neighborhood we know a lot about is Salt Lake City's Greektown. In a two-block area, there were more than sixty Greek businesses. They were located on Second South between 400 and 600 West. There were hotels, coffeehouses, saloons, grocery stores, and **import** stores. They sold octopus, Turkish tobacco, olive oil, feta cheese, liqueurs, figs, and dates.

Dr. Peter Kassinkos published a Greek language newspaper. Alex Rizos ran a drugstore and pharmacy. Andrew Dokos owned a bakery. He and his family lived upstairs. Leonidas Skliris ran a labor agency that found jobs for Greek immigrants in Utah and nearby states.

Father Markos Petrakis and his wife were part of the Greek community.
He was the first Greek priest in Carbon County.

Georgia Mageras

One of the most outstanding people in Utah's Greek neighborhood was a woman named Georgia Mageras. She was born in a small village in Greece where her father raised goats. She came to Utah with her four children in 1910. Her husband, Nick, had come earlier to find a job. When she came, there were about four thousand Greek men in Utah, but only ten women.

Georgia Mageras became very important to the Greek community. She was a doctor, a nurse, and a midwife. She delivered babies, and then she stayed afterwards to help the new mother and baby. She cooked, cleaned, washed, and answered the mother's every need, staying in the house for as long as two weeks.

Pretend you are a ten-year-old who has just arrived in Utah. You like different foods and speak a different language than most people here. You are trying to learn English to fit in with your new neighbors. Write a letter home. Tell your friends there how you feel about being in Utah.

Gorpu Miller

Mark Harnois

Discrimination

Immigrants have always faced many challenges. Many things were different in the new place than in their home lands. Some things were new and exciting. Some were hard or frightening. They often missed their own countries. They were far from their friends and families.

Sometimes, other Utahns did not like immigrants coming here. They feared that newcomers would take jobs away from them. They were nervous about people who looked different and spoke a different language. And the more different newcomers seemed, the more nervous people were.

Because of this, immigrants often met with **discrimination** in the jobs they could get and the places they could live. Their children sometimes had trouble making friends at school.

Unfortunately, blacks and people of other races faced discrimination in Utah, just as they did in the rest of the country. They had to live in certain neighborhoods. There were many cafes, hotels, and stores they could not go into. They were not allowed to stay in "white" hotels or eat at "white" restaurants. It was many years before blacks were finally allowed to go to Lagoon. They had trouble getting a high-paying job. There were laws against marriage between whites and blacks until the 1960s.

One of the worst groups ever in Utah was the Ku Klux Klan. The Ku Klux Klan was a secret organization. Its members dressed all in white. They wore robes, pointed white hats, and masks—so people would not know who they were.

People who belonged to the Ku Klux Klan thought that immigrants should be kept out of the United States. They believed immigrants only caused problems. They thought that the best people were white people who had been born in this country. They spoke out against other people. Sometimes they used violence.

There were also less obvious forms of discrimination. For a long time, many groups of people were left out of books about Utah history. It has taken a long time for people to understand that many people have worked hard to build Utah. Each group has brought new and wonderful things. Each group that comes today enriches Utah.

What Do You Think?

New people that come to Utah today continue to enrich our state. Are there children in your school you can make feel welcome in Utah? What can you do? Talk it over with other people in your class and make a list. Decide what to do first, and do it.

Can You Remember?

1. What did the stagecoaches, wagon trains, and pony express bring to Utah?

2. How did the railroad change life in Utah?

3. What was it like to work as a miner?

4. Why did people come to Utah from other countries?

5. Why did they sometimes live in separate neighborhoods?

6. What kinds of problems did immigrants have when they got here?

Geography Tie-In

1. On a world map, see how many countries you find that are in this chapter. The Chinese came from China, and Italians from Italy, and so on.

2. How many things found in nature can you find in this chapter? See who in your class can find the most.

Words to Know

communication
discrimination
ethnic
import
minerals
mosaic
ore
porter
transcontinental
transportation

Buffalo Soldiers lived in Utah at Fort Douglas and Fort Duchesne.

The Utah State Capitol Building
is in Salt Lake City.

chapter 10

A Glorious Day; Statehood

Utah became a state in 1896. One hundred years later, in 1996, Utah residents celebrated their state centennial. Becoming a state was very important. In this chapter we will talk about how that happened and what government was like in Utah after statehood.

Utah became the 45th state in the United States. Today there are fifty states.

When the pioneers first came to Utah, this region was part of Mexico. It wasn't part of the United States at all. A year later, the United States fought a war with Mexico. At the end of the war most of the West was made part of the United States. But Utah was a territory. It was not a state. Brigham Young was the first governor of the territory.

A Long Wait

The people of Utah asked Congress for statehood six different times, starting in 1849. Each time Congress said "no." Finally, in 1896, Congress granted statehood to Utah.

Why did it take so long for Utah to become a state? There were some things about Utah that Congress and people in the rest of the United States did not like. Those things had to change before Congress would let Utah become a state.

Many people who were not Mormons had a hard time living in a place where there were so many Mormons. Can you guess what some of the troubles were?

The first problem was polygamy. It was also called plural marriage. (Plural means more than one.) People who were not Mormons did not like polygamy. They thought Mormons should have just one wife at a time, like people in the rest of the country.

Brigham Young was the first governor of the Utah Territory. He was also the president of the Mormon Church at the same time.

Sugarhouse Park in Salt Lake City was once a prison. Men and a few women who were living in polygamy were sent there.

Second, many people thought Mormons had too much control. The Mormon church leaders also ran the government. People who were not Mormons wanted to help run Utah. They did not think the Mormon church should have its own political party. They wanted the Democratic and Republican parties to be in Utah, just like they were in the rest of the country. Some people also wanted other, smaller parties, like the Socialist party. People who were not Mormons also thought the church owned too many businesses, farms, and buildings. These matters greatly divided people. The two groups often had a hard time getting along. Mormons and other people often lived in separate neighborhoods and did not mix together much. They often went to separate schools. They sometimes had separate Fourth of July celebrations. They belonged to different political parties.

People across the country tried to get Mormons to change. The United States Congress passed two laws in the 1880s. They were the Edmunds Act and the Edmunds-Tucker Act. The first law made polygamy against the law. It also said that polygamists could not vote, and that women in Utah could no longer vote, either. The second law took away the Mormon church's land and buildings.

After these laws were passed, more than one thousand Utah men paid fines and went to jail for having more than one wife. Many others went into hiding to avoid arrest. That was called "going on the underground."

Mormon leaders made some changes. First, in September 1890, church President Wilford Woodruff issued a statement called the Manifesto. It said that in the future there would be no new polygamous marriages. Next, church leaders asked half the people to vote for Democrats and half to vote for Republicans. Third, the church sold many of its businesses and lands.

After all of these changes, the United States government finally said Utah could become a state. First people in Utah would have to write a state **constitution**. A constitution sets the rules for government. It tells what rights people have and what duties the government has.

Utah's Constitution

Utah's constitution was written by 107 men who had been elected to do this. They met in Salt Lake's new City and County Building in 1895. They worked for nine weeks.

Importants Parts

The Utah Constitution has several very important parts that helped Utah become a state:

- Plural marriages are "forever **prohibited**" (not allowed).
- Women have equal rights and privileges, including the right to vote and to run for office. (In most of the other states, in those days, women did not yet have the same rights as men. It took twenty more years for women to win their right to vote everywhere in the United States.)
- Church and state are separate. No church can control the government. No person should be discriminated against because of religious beliefs.

After the constitution was written, the people of Utah had to vote on it. A special election was held in the fall of 1895. Some people voted against it, but most people voted to approve it, and the constitution was adopted.

New Leaders

At the same time they voted on the state constitution, people also elected a governor and other state officials. The new governor was Heber Wells. One of the people elected to the state senate was Martha Hughes Cannon. She was the first woman ever elected to the senate of any state in the country. Her husband ran for the same office and lost.

The first female in the entire United States to be elected as a state senator was Martha Hughes Cannon.

People's Rights

The first part of Utah's constitution is a Declaration of Rights. It lists the rights that all people have. They are the same rights contained in the Bill of Rights that is part of the U.S. Constitution. The constitution says that the government will protect these rights for every person.

These rights include:

Freedom of religion: You can worship the way you and your family decide, or not at all.

Freedom of speech: You can say your feelings about any subject without being arrested (but it can't cause danger to others). You can even criticize the government.

Freedom of assembly: You can join and meet with any group. However, you cannot commit crimes with that group.

Freedom of petition: You can write to those you have elected to public office, such as a senator, a mayor, or the governor. You can ask them to vote in a certain way.

Statehood at Last!

On January 4, 1896, Grover Cleveland, the president of the United States, signed a paper that made Utah the 45th state.

Governor Wells, the first governor of the new state, gave a long speech in the Salt Lake Tabernacle. In Salt Lake City a large steam whistle sounded from the tower of the City and County Building, adding to the noise created by shotguns, cannons, bells, fireworks, shouting, and a parade.

At 9:13 a.m. Superintendent Brown of Western Union rushed from his office armed with a shotgun and fired two shots into the air, signaling the news. A small boy in the vicinity dived for cover thinking a robbery was in progress. . . .

The news spread like wildfire throughout the territory and frantic committees put into motion planned festivities to mark the event. Monday after the signing day was a public holiday "for thanksgiving and rejoicing." All schools were closed.

—Utah Historical Quarterly, 1995, Volume 63-4

Evan Stephens composed Utah's state song, "Utah, We Love Thee." He also wrote many other songs and was conductor of the Mormon Tabernacle Choir.

The *Deseret News* asked every city and town to decorate their homes in honor of statehood day. Red, white, and blue banners appeared on walls and in windows of homes, churches, and businesses.

The Salt Lake Tabernacle was also decorated with a star lit with electric lights. The star was still hanging when this picture was taken of the Mormon Tabernacle Choir a few years later.

People all over the state celebrated. Here is what happened in some of Utah's towns:

A reporter in Manti wrote that Wilford Woodruff said the noise was like a "Fourth of July in the winter time" as people went out into the streets on the cold but sunny winter day to join the fun. They jingled cow and sheep bells, set off dynamite, and fired rifles.

In Fillmore, just a half-hour after dancers left a ball, the building burst into flames. "Where but a short time previous had been joy and mer[r]iment. . . ," now there were just ashes. An exploding lamp had caused the fire.

At Corinne someone rang the courthouse bell so hard that it cracked.

In Tooele and Lehi people hung pictures of early pioneers on church walls. There were flags everywhere.

In Park City, 150 children and teens formed their own parade and marched through the streets of the mining town making "more noise than had been seen or heard here in many a day." They sang at businesses, and received nuts and candy.

The Union Pacific Railroad offered round-trip tickets to Salt Lake City for one fare on Inauguration Day.

In Ogden, gentlemen were charged 25 cents for the dance, but ladies were admitted free.

Children of the Kamas schools were given a free sleigh ride as they listened to music by the Kamas Brass band.

People in Gunnison ended their celebration by yelling three cheers and "a tiger," while waving their handkerchiefs. A tiger was a great growl at the end of the cheers.

In Clarkston, men at a dance invented forty-five new dance steps.

On January 4th, 1996, Utahns celebrated 100 years of statehood.

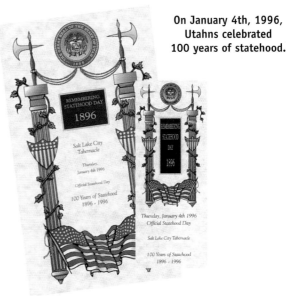

Government for the People

Government is the rules people work out for living together. Your school may have a student government. Large countries and small groups all have governments. There are many different kinds.

Different countries in the world have different governments. The kind that exists in the United States is only one kind. It makes sense to us. Other governments make sense to other people.

The United States is a representative democracy. It is run by **representatives**. Instead of all the people voting for the laws, the people elect representatives to vote for them. The people still have the power and the final authority. If the representatives don't vote the way the people want them to, they can vote for someone else next time.

These are the state's first representatives in 1896. Martha Cannon is the second woman from the left. The other woman was a clerk.

Activity
Role Play Democracy at Work

Let's see how representative democracy works.

Choose a subject that is important to people in Utah. It might be one of these three: Should Utah have year-round schools? Should Utah have a nuclear power plant? Should taxes be raised? Maybe there is another issue you are concerned about.

Divide into small groups to talk separately about the subject. Then take a vote to see what ideas your group favors. Next, take a vote to choose someone from the group to be your representative. The representatives from each group get together to talk about the issue. Each representative will tell the others what the people in his or her group thought. Then the representatives will vote about what to do.

Get Involved!

There are two things to remember about our system of government. First, the people have a right to be involved. Second, in order for it to work the way it is supposed to, the people must be involved in it. They have to take part. That means all of the people—male and female, people of all races, rich and poor, people from here and people from other countries—everyone has a right to be involved.

Voting and Political Parties

In our government, representatives are chosen during elections by a vote of the people. Who can vote? Anyone can vote who is a citizen of the United States, is at least eighteen years old, and is registered (signed up).

Anyone over age eighteen can also run for office. For certain offices different ages are required. The president of the United States must be at least thirty-five years old, but an eighteen-year-old can run for a city council. Tab Uno was elected to the Salt Lake City School Board when he was eighteen and a student at the University of Utah.

For some offices a person must first be nominated (named) by one of the political parties. Political parties are groups of people who have a lot of the same ideas about government. Most people belong to either the Democratic or the Republican Party. Those are the two major parties in Utah and in the rest of the United States. Their job is to get their people voted into office.

Republican   Democrat

There are also third parties. Not as many people belong to them, but third parties are important. They give people more candidates and ideas to choose from. Sometimes the two major parties use some third party ideas to win more votes. Third parties have had great influence in American history. Utah has a strong third party tradition. In the early 1900s, the Socialist party was a strong third party in Utah and elected many people to office.

As another choice, some citizens do not belong to any party. They run for office or vote as **independents**.

Once people have been chosen to run for office, they are called candidates. Political party workers and friends try to win votes for their candidates. They raise money, make posters, buy TV advertising, and give speeches.

> **Both male and female citizens of this State shall enjoy equally all civil, political and religious rights and privileges.**
>
> —*Constitution of the State of Utah,* ARTICLE IV, SECTION I

Taking Part in Government

Citizens have a right and a duty to take part in their government. Only they can make a representative democracy work. What can they do?

- Vote.
- Run for office.
- Tell your representatives and council members what you want them to do (by letter, fax, E-mail, telephone, or in person).
- Write letters to the editor of newspapers to tell other people how you feel.
- Hand out brochures and leaflets to people.
- Get the facts (from newspapers, magazines, TV and radio reports).
- Learn about the candidates running for office at voting time (from leaflets, newspapers, speeches, TV and radio).
- Take part in meetings, marches, protests.
- Give speeches.

Branches of Government

Utah's constitution outlines a government with three distinct branches, or parts. These are the *legislative*, *executive*, and *judicial* branches. Each branch has certain jobs to do. No branch can do the work of the other branches. This is called "separation of powers." The idea is that no one person or group should hold all the power. The power is divided.

Can you figure out the job of each branch?
1. Which branch legislates (makes the laws)?
2. Which branch judges the fairness of laws and interprets (explains) them?
3. Which branch executes (uses) the laws to govern the people?

Branches of Government each have special jobs. This is called "balance of power."

If you answered 1) legislative, 2) judicial, 3) executive, you were correct.

Executive Branch

The governor heads the executive branch of a state. Governors are chosen by direct vote of all the people. Since it became a state, Utah has elected as governor Democrats twelve times and Republicans thirteen times.

Utah's governors can be men or women, but Utah has never elected a woman to serve as governor. Other states have had female governors. Would you vote for a woman for governor? Why or why not?

The governor's term is four years. Governors can run for re-election as many times as they want, but only one of Utah's governors was elected more than two times. He was a Democrat named Calvin Rampton. People liked him so much he was elected three times.

Here is a list of some jobs the governor does. Which do you think are the most important?

- Sees that the laws of the state are carried out
- Is the chief of the state militia (army)
- Suggests **bills** to the legislature
- Gives a state **budget** (costs for a year) to the legislature
- Signs bills into law or **vetoes** (rejects) them
- Calls the legislature into special (extra) sessions
- Can grant a **pardon** (forgiveness) to people found guilty of crime. It may keep them out of jail!

Utah's governor Mike Leavitt and his wife Jacalyn Smith Leavitt in 1996, Utah's Centennial Year. The Governor is head of the state executive branch.

Judicial Branch

The state judicial branch is made up of several levels of courts where judges **interpret** (explain) the laws. They say how laws fit each case that comes to court. They decide if laws follow the constitution. If they don't, the judges say the laws are **unconstitutional**, and they are erased from the law books.

Courts also judge whether or not people are guilty of breaking any laws. If people have broken the law, courts decide how they should be punished.

Different kinds of crimes are tried in different courts. The highest state court is called the supreme court. If people don't like what happened in a lower court, they can take their case to the next higher court. The Utah State Supreme Court is the final word in Utah.

Honorable Christine Durham serves as chief justice on the Utah Supreme Court.

Legislative Branch

The job of the legislative branch is to make the laws. The state legislature is made up of two parts, called houses—the House of Representatives and the Senate. Representatives and Senators are voted into office by the people.

Legislators live in their hometowns and go to Salt Lake City when the legislature meets. It meets every year for forty-five days beginning in January. It may also be called back into a special session later in the year if the governor thinks there is more work to do.

How a Bill Becomes a Law

When the legislature is working at the state **capitol** building in Salt Lake City people can go and watch. Legislators divide into groups to study bills. A bill is a written idea for a new law. Legislators talk about and vote on bills. When a majority (more than half) of both the representatives and senators vote for the bill, it goes to the governor.

The governor can either sign it into law or veto it. A veto means to say "no" to the bill. If the governor does nothing, the bill becomes law. If the governor vetoes it, the senators and representatives can vote again. If two-thirds of the legislators vote for the bill again, the bill becomes a law, even though the governor doesn't want it to.

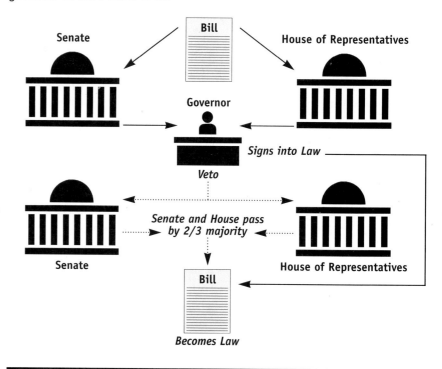

Local Government Services

There are two kinds of **local** government—city and county. Local means close to home. Besides making laws, local governments provide many different services to their people.

Utah's state constitution gives city and county governments the power to collect taxes. That money pays for the services local governments provide.

Taxes pay for the services of sheriff, police, and fire departments. Taxes pay for building local streets and plowing snow. Local governments run schools and libraries with tax money.

Counties keep records of marriages and births. They also provide health services. For free, or for a few dollars, people can get a flu shot or a well-baby checkup at the local health office.

Cities arrange for a clean water supply for houses and businesses, and pick up garbage.

Photo by Bill Willcox ▶

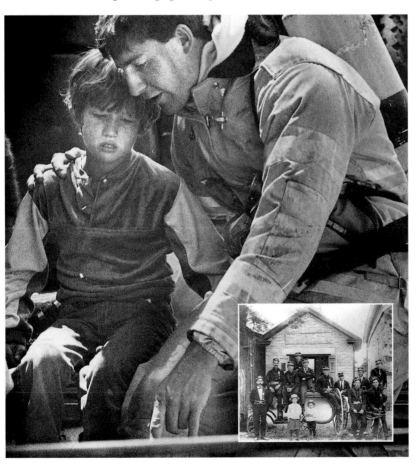

The fire department is a service of the local government.
The photo at the right is the Tooele Fire Department long ago, and at the left is a modern fireman helping a child after a home fire.

Financing the State

Where the money comes from:
Income tax, Gas tax, Property tax, Sales tax, Corporation income tax, Social Security tax, Estate and gift tax, License fees

Where the money goes:
Farm programs, Health care, Postal service, Social Security Unemployment, Interest on debts, Public welfare, Highways

Schools

Police and fire protection

Road work

Libraries

Parks

Utah Counties and County Seats

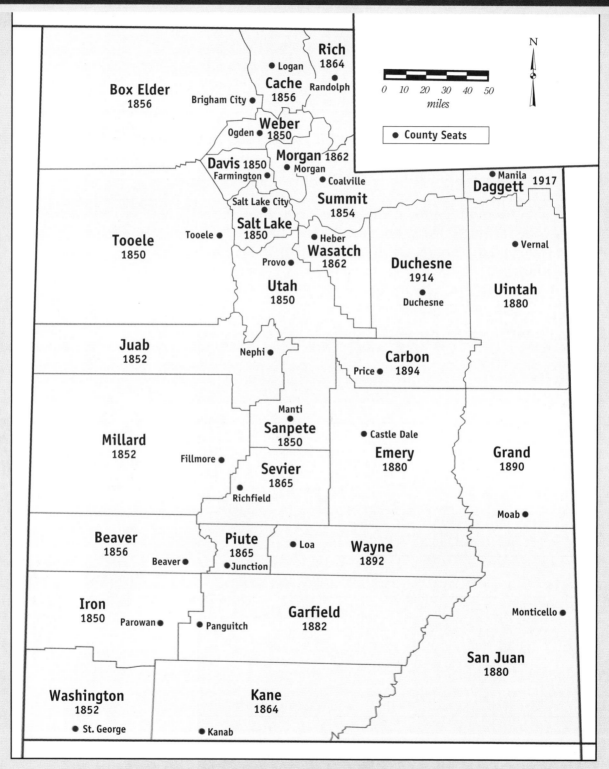

N

| | | | | | |
|0|10|20|30|40|50|

miles

● County Seats

Box Elder 1856

● Logan

Rich 1864

Cache 1856

● Randolph

Brigham City ●

Weber 1850

Ogden ●

Morgan 1862

● Morgan

Davis 1850

Farmington ●

● Coalville

Salt Lake City ●

Summit 1854

Manila ●

Daggett 1917

Tooele 1850

Tooele ●

Salt Lake 1850

● Heber

Wasatch 1862

Provo ●

Duchesne 1914

● Duchesne

● Vernal

Uintah 1880

Utah 1850

Juab 1852

Nephi ●

Carbon 1894

Price ●

Manti ●

Sanpete 1850

● Castle Dale

Emery 1880

Grand 1890

Millard 1852

Fillmore ●

Sevier 1865

Richfield ●

Moab ●

Beaver 1856

Beaver ●

Piute 1865

● Junction

● Loa

Wayne 1892

Iron 1850

Parowan ●

● Panguitch

Garfield 1882

Monticello ●

San Juan 1880

Washington 1852

● St. George

Kane 1864

● Kanab

Utah is divided into government regions called counties. Each county has a county government.
The people in the counties must also live the laws of the Utah State and the United States government.
The county seat is a city in each county where the government offices are. The dates on the map are
the year each county was organized. Locate your county on the map. What is your county seat?

What Do you Think?
Talk about these things with your class.
1. Do you think it is good that religion and government are kept separate?
2. Why do you think that for many years women in the United States could not vote?
3. What makes a democracy a good government for the United States?

Can You Remember?
1. Name two political parties.
2. In what year did Utah become the 45th state?
3. What kind of government does the United States have? What does that name mean?
4. What is a constitution?
5. Name the three branches of government and tell what each does.
6. How does the government get money?
7. What are some things government does with the money?

Geography Tie-In
1. On a world map, find the country of Mexico. Most of the land in the West, including Utah, was once owned by Mexico. List on the board some of the things that would be the same, and some things that might be different in your life if we were still a part of Mexico.
2. Do some research and find out which states were made states after Utah. There were five. Locate them on a map.

Words to Know
bill
budget
capitol (hint: it is spelled with an "o" because it has a d<u>o</u>me on it)
constitution
independent
interpret
local
pardon
prohibit
representative
unconstitutional
veto

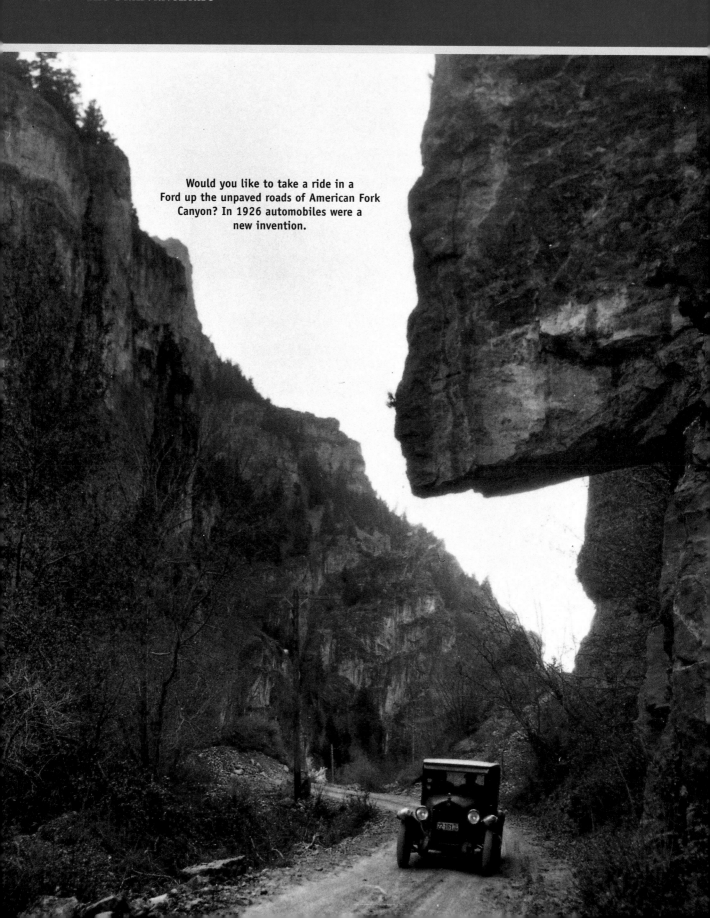

Would you like to take a ride in a Ford up the unpaved roads of American Fork Canyon? In 1926 automobiles were a new invention.

Inventions, Industry, Depression and War

In the years after statehood in 1896, Utah became modern. It was more and more a part of the rest of the United States. The things that happened in other parts of the country also happened in Utah. Utah entered the twentieth century.

The Growth of Cities and Industry

Once Utah was a state of farms and small towns. Then more and more it became a state of cities. By the 1920s a majority of people in Utah lived in cities.

Like the rest of the country, Utah also became more and more a state of factory and mine workers. Gold, silver, iron, copper, and coal have been the state's most important minerals.

Even though more and more people lived in cities and worked in businesses, factories, and mines, farming was still important. Many Utah farmers continued to grow the food people needed. They sold it to people in Utah and outside of the state. By 1920 the largest crop was sugar beets. Dairy farms and cattle and sheep ranches were also important.

Academy Avenue in Provo in the early part of the 1900s.

Copper mining in Bingham Canyon
has been big business for over
one hundred years.

Today Kennecott Copper Company, in Salt Lake County, is Utah's biggest mining company. It provides copper for electrical wires and motors. The copper is also used in automobiles, CD players, computers, plumbing pipes, and, of course, copper pennies.

More people in Utah began to work in factories. Utah factories made all kinds of products—furniture, parts for airplanes, toys, clothing, shoes—almost anything you can think of.

People in Utah also worked more and more in offices and businesses. They sold things to people—in department stores, drug stores, and grocery stores.

▲ The more cities there were, the more stores there were.
This store is in Park City.

▼ Women started working outside their homes more.
This is the American Linen Laundry in Salt Lake City.

Today Utah's newest
factories make high-tech
products, such as
computers, calculators,
and watches.

In the early 1900s, many of Utah's new workers were
women. They started leaving their homes to get jobs. Today
most women work outside the home sometime during their
lives. Women used to work mainly in certain jobs. They
were teachers, nurses, secretaries, and store clerks. Those
are important jobs, and many women still work at them.
Now men work at those jobs, too.

Now women also work at many other jobs. Women are
doctors, lawyers, truck drivers, engineers, business man-
agers, repair people, electricians, and computer program-
mers. Women in Utah work at every kind of job there is.

Problems

Growth of cities and **industries** caused many problems. People began to think about what to do to solve them. They saw many things that needed to be changed. There was **poverty**, child labor, long working hours, dirty and dangerous working places, dirty streets, unsafe water, unsafe food, no garbage collection, and no street cleaning.

Most early cities had dirty streets and yards. When Utah became a state, there was no garbage collection in cities. Garbage piled up in yards. Dead animals decayed at the sides of the road. There were no indoor bathrooms—people used outhouses. Streets were not paved. They were muddy in the winter and spring. Sometimes the mud was a foot deep. In the summer the streets were dusty. People choked when they walked across them.

Ogden and other cities were not the cleanest places to live.

Laws Made Things Better

Here are some things that people did to solve the problems at home and at work. They passed laws so that:

- Bosses in the mining industry could not make people work more than eight hours a day.
- Companies could not make women and children work more than nine hours a day, or fifty-four hours a week.
- Children under the age of fourteen could not work in mines.
- Workers could not be fired for joining a labor union. (We will discuss labor unions in the next chapter.)
- A state board of health was created.
- Bosses had to pay their workers no less than a certain amount of money.
- Mines had to have rules for safety.
- Workers hurt on the job would still get paid.
- Milk sold in stores would have to be fresh.
- Companies could not pollute air and water.
- Cities would collect garbage regularly.
- Cities would pave their streets with **asphalt** and clean them regularly.
- Cities would put in the sewer systems needed for indoor bathrooms.

Milk sold in stores would have to be clean and fresh.

Cities would have to collect garbage regularly.

Cities would put in the sewer systems needed for indoor bathrooms. At that time most people had outhouses.

A new law said boys under the age of fourteen could not work in the mines.

A New Invention

When baseball's World Series was shown in 1947, television became popular. For many years before that, inventors had been working in different countries to develop it. People already had radios, but they wanted to see programs in their own homes. A Utah man, Philo Farnsworth, invented an important part of early television. He was the first to make it all electronic. There is a statue of Philo Farnsworth in the United States Capitol in Washington, D.C.

Stoves burned coal and wood before electricity was available.

Inventions

Many inventions changed people's lives. Electricity was one of the most important. It changed the way people worked, played, and lived.

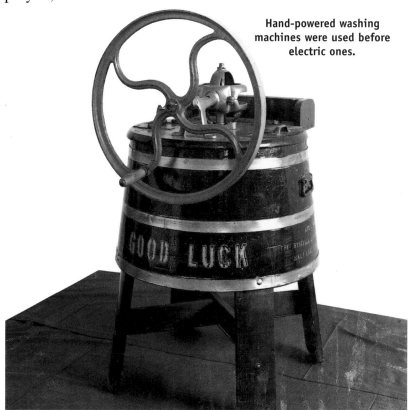

Hand-powered washing machines were used before electric ones.

Electricity

Machines for making electricity are called generators. That is why we sometimes say that we generate electricity. Generators were invented only about one hundred years ago. After that, it was possible to have electric lights. Then new machines were invented that used electricity. There were electric washing machines, irons, stoves, refrigerators, and vacuum cleaners.

The first public display of electric lights in Utah was in the summer of 1880. The circus came to town. It was called W. W. Cole's Great Concorporation of Circus, Menagerie, Aquarium, and Congress of Living Wonders. It performed in Salt Lake City and then traveled to Ogden, Brigham City, and Logan before moving on to California. It performed under electric lights powered by its own generator. The *Deseret News* said the lights "emitted a soft and brilliant lustre like magnified moonlight."

Soon after the circus came, a company was formed to put electric lights on Salt Lake City streets. The new lights made a big difference. Before electric lights, there were gas lights. They were not very bright. Downtown Salt Lake was very dark at night, and streets were not safe for walking. One man said, "I started out one evening to see my best girl. It was so dark I fell over fourteen rock piles and seven wire fences." Most people stayed home at night and traveled the streets only in the daytime. Electricity changed that.

Automobiles

After 1920 automobiles became very popular. The first automobiles cost about $500. The price was reasonable, and many people bought them. The first cars came in only a few styles and colors. Henry Ford owned the factory that made Ford cars. He joked that people could have any color of car they wanted, as long as it was black.

Before automobiles, horses and mules and other work animals were used for transportation. Stables took care of horses, for hire. Stable owners fed the horses, brushed them, and provided stalls for them to sleep in. Blacksmith shops were needed to make horseshoes. There were businesses to make saddles and harnesses. Other shops made the wagons that horses pulled. With the coming of the automobile, those businesses were not needed as much. New ones were. What were they?

People fell in love with the automobile. This is an auto club at Lagoon in 1908.

Radio

Two of the most exciting inventions were the radio and the movies. All across the United States, the radio was awesome. Everyone wanted to buy one. The trouble was, at first there were not enough to go around. People visited the houses of friends lucky enough to own one. From all over a neighborhood people gathered to listen to their favorite programs. They were amazed. Imagine hearing voices and music that came from the air! Before long everyone had to have a radio.

The whole family liked to gather around to hear the radio.

The first radio station in Utah was KZN. It was on the roof of the Deseret News Building in downtown Salt Lake City. Later it changed its call letters to KSL. At first it was on only one-half hour a day, from 8:00 P.M. to 8:30 P.M.

Moving Picture Shows

The first movies were silent, with no talking or music. Then "talkies" came in, with sound. To go to a movie cost twenty-five cents for adults and ten cents for children. Soon everyone was going.

At first movie theaters were small, but soon large, fancy theaters were built. They were like palaces. In fact, Salt Lake City's Capitol Theatre was called a motion picture palace.

The Lyric Theater in Salt Lake City had a cry room, or nursery, where parents could leave their babies while they watched the movie. There was a nurse in the ladies rest room in case someone got sick.

Not only were movies shown in Utah, they were made here, too. Because of its wonderful scenery, southern Utah was a favorite site. The first movie made in Utah was a western starring Tom Mix. He was one of the most popular cowboy stars of the time.

Theaters had plush seats and walls lined with imitation gold. Ceilings were two or three stories high. Inside the theater were ushers in uniforms with brass buttons and gold braid. The ushers led the way to vacant seats with their flashlights.

Ask some older people if they remember the Lyric, or the Pantages Theater and the Orpheum Theater in Salt Lake; or the Egyptian in Ogden, or the Egyptian in Gunnison.

The Capitol Theater in Salt Lake City is still used today for ballet, opera, and live theater. This photo was taken in 1937.

New Inventions Come to Utah

INVENTION	FIRST USED IN U.S.	FIRST USED IN UTAH
Telephone	1875	1878
Light Bulbs	1879	1881; Salt Lake City and Ogden
Power Plants	1879	1881; Salt Lake City
Lights in Schools	1879	1881; Salt Lake City
Electric Streetcars	1887	1889; Salt Lake City
Automobiles	1900	1900; 20 cars sold in Salt Lake City
Airplanes	1903; 1923, 1st coast-to-coast flight	1927; 1st flight to Utah
Radio	1906	1922
Movies	1905	1905

Look at when the inventions were first used in the U.S. Then see when they were used in Utah.

One woman at Saltair said, "I always wore a bathing cap and put a clean handkerchief underneath it. And that was so if you got a dose of salt you would have a clean handkerchief to wipe your eyes."

Outdoor Fun

Besides radio and movies, there were other new forms of entertainment. Baseball games became popular. Every small town had its own team. Many companies also had teams.

Pleasure resorts were popular, too. Now we call them amusement parks. Saltair and Lagoon were the largest.

Saltair was on the south shore of the Great Salt Lake. People went there to swim in the lake. The water was so salty they didn't sink, but floated like corks. But they had to be careful not to get salt in their eyes. That would really sting.

Saltair also had one of the largest dance floors in the world. There was a band at each end. When one stopped playing the other began, so that the music never stopped.

Couples danced the first and last dance with each other and changed partners in between. Those who danced cheek-to-cheek were asked to leave the floor.

People went to Lagoon to relax and take a boat ride on the lake.

Saltair Resort was built in 1893. It burned down in 1925.
This is how it looked after it was rebuilt.

A man called "Professor" William Woodward gave free dance lessons. "Before the summer is over," he said, "more people in Salt Lake will be dancing the new and modern steps than in any western city."

Saltair also had the world's highest roller coaster at that time. It was called The Race Through the Clouds. There were also movies, bicycle races, roller skating, and nickel-in-the-slot machines. There were bull fights, wild west shows, and an alligator farm.

Lagoon had a lake, called a lagoon. Its first thrill ride was the Shoot-the-Chutes, a distant cousin of today's log flume.

Utah Follows the Country into War

World War I

In 1914 World War I began in Europe. Nearly three years later, the United States declared war on Germany. It was an awful war. The world had never seen a war that was so **destructive**. Utah men served as soldiers. Utah women served as nurses and ambulance drivers.

On the home front, there was loyal support for the war. Women worked in the Red Cross and as army nurses. Families planted gardens so more food could be sent to the armies in Europe. Schools gave children prizes for growing the largest vegetables. Children also saved dimes to give to the war effort.

In 1918 the war ended. We welcomed our soldiers home. We hoped never again to fight another war like it.

Red Cross nurses marched in a war fund parade to raise money for World War I.

The Great Depression

A major event in Utah history was the Great Depression of the 1930s.

A depression is a time when most people can't make enough money to take care of their families. They want to work, but they can't find jobs. The depression of the 1930s was the worst depression the United States has ever known. That is why it is called the Great Depression.

A major reason for the depression was that people were not paid enough for the work they did. They could not afford to buy things. Another reason was making too much, or growing too much, of something. Farmers grew too much food. Therefore, people could not buy up all the crops. Then the farmers did not earn enough money.

Factories also made more goods than people could buy. They fired some of their workers. Then the workers had even less money to buy what they needed. Stores and factories closed, and thousands of people lost their jobs.

In one school, a teacher asked a girl, "What's wrong with you?"

"I'm just hungry," the girl said.

"You may go home and eat," the teacher said.

"I can't," the child answered. "Today it is my sister's turn to eat."

People traded things they owned for other things they needed. People grew gardens in their backyards. They saved everything they could. They mended old clothes again and again to make them last longer. When people's shoes got holes in the bottom, they put cardboard inside.

> "I did what I had to do. I always seemed to find a way to make things work. We just did what we had to do, just one day at a time."
>
> —*A young mother during the depression*

Depression Cycle

Factories lay off workers

People lose their jobs

People cannot buy things

Stores go out of business

Stores do not order from factories

Factories do not get orders

Churches tried to help. The Catholic Women's League, the Jewish Relief, and the Protestant Ladies Aid Society helped people get food and shelter. The LDS Church began a welfare program so people could get food and clothing by working for the church. They started farms to grow food for people who needed it.

The Great Depression lasted much longer than people thought it would. It lasted more than ten years.

During the depression, people lined up to get free food from the government.

The New Deal

The federal government tried to end the depression and help people. The things it did are called the New Deal.

As part of the New Deal, older people received retirement money called Social Security from the government. It gave loans to farmers. Young people were trained for jobs. Children received free school lunches.

Government work projects were started in every state. Thousands of people got jobs with a government program called the Works Progress Administration (WPA). In Utah the WPA built roads, sidewalks, and hospitals. It built schools, parks, and playgrounds. It built sewers and water lines. Almost every town in Utah had government work projects.

There was a work program called the Civilian Conservation Corps (CCC). Under it the government hired young men to work in forests and build bridges, picnic tables, and campgrounds.

The government tried many things to end the depression. Even with all the help, the Great Depression continued. Then World War II came, and people got jobs in the army and navy, and in factories to make war goods. With the beginning of World War II the depression ended.

The Great Depression had a big influence on people. People saw the importance of helping each other during hard times. They also saw that government could be helpful in their lives.

A hot lunch program was started in city schools. Classes in nutrition were offered to parents. Adult education programs were set up in city schools.

Work projects in many places gave people jobs.

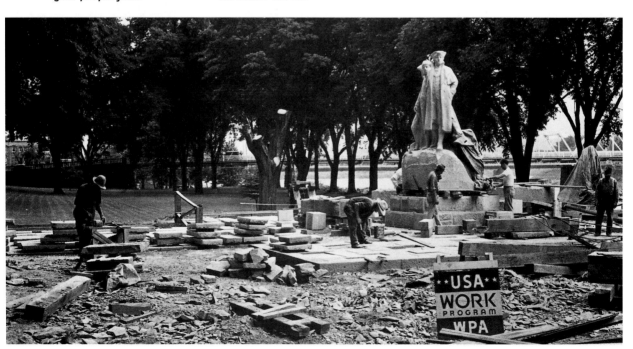

World War II

In 1939 a second world war began in Europe. The United States did not get involved for two years. Then we declared war on Germany and Japan. The war lasted until 1945. It ended when we dropped two atomic bombs on Japan.

During World War II, things were not as hard in the United States as they were in some countries. That is because the war was not fought here. The fighting went on in other places. Even so, the war changed things here. More than 65,000 Utah men and women served in the war. Almost 1,500 of them were killed.

More women went to work for wages outside the home. Many of them worked at jobs men used to do. People found out that women were good truck drivers, aircraft mechanics, welders, machinists, and carpenters. Children also did their part. They collected pots, pans, and tin cans that could be turned into metal for making ships.

Women went to work to help the war effort. This picture was taken in 1943.

Ration coupons had to be used to buy certain things at the store. These belonged to Beth Gerrard Allen. Her husband, brother, and brothers-in-law were in the air force in Texas and overseas. She worked on airplanes that would be sent overseas for the war.

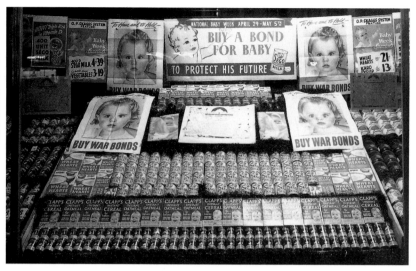

War bonds were sold to make money for the war effort overseas.

Factories everywhere stopped making the usual things and started to make war goods. Car factories turned out tanks. Typewriter factories made machine guns. Vacuum cleaner factories made bullets. The Geneva Steel Works in Orem made steel for battleships. A factory in Manti made parachutes.

Just like people everywhere in the United States, Utahns had to put up with empty store shelves. It was hard to get such things as coffee, hairpins, nylon stockings, and alarm clocks. Not as many of those things were being made. It was more important to make bullets and other war goods. Some goods were sent to the soldiers overseas. If the people here complained, storekeepers had an answer: "Don't you know there's a war on?"

One way to save things that were scarce was to "ration" or share them. People could buy only so much sugar, meat, butter, coffee, gas, and tires. Each family was given ration stamps every month to use to buy these things. When their stamps ran out, they could not buy them until the next month when they would get more stamps.

Topaz War Camp

One of the saddest parts of World War II in Utah was the holding of Japanese Americans in a camp called Topaz. Utah was one of ten places in the United States where Japanese Americans were forced to live during the war. They were American citizens, and they were loyal to the United States. Still people feared they might help the Japanese. So they were made to leave their homes.

Children living at Topaz went to school, planted gardens, and made friends there.

My Mom, Pop, and Me

My Mom, Pop, and me
Us living three
Dreaded the day
When we rode away,
Away to the land
With lots of sand
My mom, pop, and me.

The day of evacuation
We left our little station
Leaving our friends
And my tree that bends
Away to the land
With lots of sand
My mom, pop, and me.
—*Itsuko Taniguchi, 1943*

About 8,000 people were brought to Topaz near Delta. Life was hard there. Topaz had wooden barracks where people lived together. Around the camp was barbed wire. There were watchtowers with armed guards.

After the war, people began to realize that doing this to Japanese American citizens was a mistake. They realized that loyalty could not be measured by race or skin color.

Effects of World War II in Utah

Utah's population continued to grow and become more **diverse**. Many new people moved into the state to take jobs. The population of Hispanics increased greatly. Companies did not just wait for Hispanics to apply for jobs. They asked for them, because they were such good workers. Some of them were the first Puerto Rican people to come to Utah. Many of them stayed after the war ended.

The population of African Americans also grew, and they continued to meet with discrimination. When a famous jazz singer named Ella Fitzgerald came to Salt Lake, she was not allowed to stay at the Hotel Utah because of her color.

A man named Billy Mason is a barber in Salt Lake City. He says that blacks could not go many places in those days:

> *Here, and just about everywhere else in those days, black people didn't have any place to go bowling, you know. Oh, there was a Normandy Skating Rink on Sixth South and Main. The only time we could go roller skating there was from 12 o'clock at night until 1:00. One hour. Yeah. We couldn't eat at certain restaurants, or get into certain social clubs. . . .*

A breakthrough in Utah came because of Robert Freed and Ranch Kimball. They took over Lagoon, and also the

Polynesians are people who come here from islands in the Pacific Ocean. They began coming here as converts to the Mormon church in about 1965. Most of them today come looking for work, or because they have friends or family here. The largest group is from Tonga. Others are from Samoa, New Zealand, Hawaii, and Tahiti.

Dancers from the Pacific Islands wear colorful costumes.

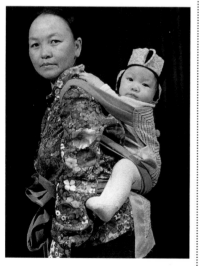

Some of Utah's new immigrants come from Laos, Thailand, Cambodia, or other countries in Southeast Asia. This Hmong mother carries her baby on her back.

Terrace Ballroom in downtown Salt Lake City. Blacks had not been able to go to these places. The new owners welcomed everyone of every background and color to attend. And people like Danny W. Burnett and Albert Fritz led protests against stores that would not serve blacks at lunch counters.

Other Wars

Since the end of World War II, Utahns have fought in other wars the United States has been involved in—including the Korean War, the Vietnam War, and wars in the Middle East.

The longest and most unpopular war in U.S. history was the Vietnam War. Nearly 28,000 Utahns fought in that war. In 1969, more than 4,000 people marched to protest the war in Vietnam. They marched down South Temple Street to the Federal Building in downtown Salt Lake City. It was the largest anti-war march ever held in Utah.

Recent Immigrants

Since the end of World War II, people have kept coming to Utah to live. The latest group to come to Utah are from Southeast Asia. They have come from Vietnam, Thailand, Laos, and Cambodia. They started coming in 1975 after the war ended in Vietnam. In their countries, most of them lived on farms and grew their own crops. They did not speak English when they came, and most were Buddhists. It has been very hard for them to get used to their new life here.

The story of a Southeast Asian immigrant might sound like this:

I am ten years old. My brother and I escaped from Cambodia. We had to run and hide in the jungle until we got to the ocean. Ten of our family started, but only four of us made it. When we got to the water, we had to pay hundreds of dollars to get on a small boat. We had little food and no belongings. We did not have enough money for all of us, so some had to stay behind. We hope to earn enough money to send for the others soon. It has been hard to get used to our new life here.

End of a Century

Larger cities, electricity, automobiles, new laws, wars, the depression, and civil rights—the twentieth century brought many changes to life in Utah.

What Do You Think?

In small groups, discuss these things:

1. What things caused our population to grow? In what ways is population growth good and in what ways can it be bad?

2. What inventions do you think have helped people the most? Why?

3. What are some ways people can get by on less money if they need to? Is this important?

Can You Remember?

1. What problems did people living in cities have?

2. What problems did workers have?

3. What kind of solutions were tried for the cities and the workers?

4. What were five inventions that changed people's lives in the early 1900s?

5. Name the two large wars Utahns fought in.

6. What can you remember about the Great Depression?

7. Why was the New Deal started?

8. What group of people were kept at Topaz?

Geography Tie-in

1. On a world map in your room, see if you can find all of the countries on page 196 after the heading "Recent Immigrants." What continent are they on? What ocean did the people have to cross to get to America?

2. Use books in your library to find something interesting about one of the countries. What kind of a place is it? What is the land like? What kinds of animals live there? How do the people live? Make a book about the country.

Words to Know

asphalt

destructive

diverse

industry

poverty

Newsboys in 1907 delivered the Christmas *Deseret News* to earn money.

chapter 12

Economics in Utah and the United States

People have needs. They also have wants. They need food, clothing, and shelter. They want things like cars, books, toys, and bicycles. These are called **goods**, or **products**. They need medical care from doctors and nurses. They need education from teachers. They may want help repairing their washing machine or fixing a broken window. These are called **services**. **Economics** is the study of how people get the goods and services that they need and want.

An **economic system** is a way of producing and selling the goods and services people need and want. There are many different economic systems. Different countries in the world use different systems. The United States has what is called a **capitalistic**, or **free enterprise**, economic system. Here is how it works:

Some people in the United States own the factories and companies that produce goods and services. And because they own them, they can run them the way they want. The business is the property of the owner. Owners plan the businesses. Owners decide what to produce, and how much to charge for it. They decide where to do business. They decide who they want to help them. They are in charge of selling the product, too.

Business owners hire other people, called **employees**, to work for them. The owner pays the employees a **wage**, or a **salary**. Most adults in the United States are employees.

Before Utah was part of the United States, it had its own money system. What can you learn about Utah by looking at the money?

Making a Profit

How do business owners make money? Usually they sell what the workers produce. They can sell goods or a service. The electric company sells electricity. Dentists sell their services to fix your teeth.

The money left after expenses are subtracted is called a **profit**. People who make shoes have to pay for the leather, the glue, the machines, and the building. They have to pay themselves for all the work in making the shoes. They must sell the shoes for more than it costs to make them. If not, they will have a loss instead of a profit. They will soon be out of business!

Owners want their workers to come on time, work hard, and do good work. They want them to be trained for the job. They don't want workers to steal supplies from them, or waste time.

Workers expect the company to pay them fairly, provide medical insurance and vacation pay, and to provide clean, safe places to work.

Price, Supply and Demand

How do business owners decide how much to charge buyers for their product? The selling price depends on a lot of things. The price has to be more than what it cost the company to make the item, so the business will make a profit. Sometimes the price also depends on how much of something there is. If a toy becomes so popular that a company cannot make enough for everyone who wants it, the company can sell the toy for a higher price. People will be willing to pay more to get it. This is called the law of supply and demand.

Sometimes a company has to lower its prices. Maybe a company makes bicycles and tries to sell them at a certain price. People don't buy very many of them. Then the company has a lot of extra bicycles sitting around. They might lower the price to get people to buy them. Or maybe there are two companies that make bicycles. One of the companies might lower their price to get people to buy from them instead of the other company.

Sometimes there is only one company that produces a certain product. If buyers want that product or service, they will have to pay whatever price the company charges.

Making and selling shoes is one way of earning a profit.

When there is a lot of something, the cost can be lower. If there is not very much of something, the cost is usually higher.

Consumers Buy Products and Services

People are workers. They are also consumers. A **consumer** is a person who buys things. Anyone who spends money is a consumer. Are you a consumer? You are if you buy things. What kinds of things do you buy with your money?

Most people want to spend their money wisely. They compare different brands to get the best for their money. They also compare prices at different stores.

Stores try to get consumers to shop in their stores by advertising. Advertising may be on the radio, on TV, on billboards beside the highways and on the sides of buildings. You see and hear it everywhere. Being a wise consumer means understanding how advertising works.

Have you ever bought something because the advertisements made it seem exciting? And then you found out it wasn't? It seemed like the commercial lied. Do you believe everything a commercial says?

Here are some methods used in advertising to get you to buy:

1. Color and excitement. The ad is bright and colorful so people will notice it. The product seems fun and exciting.

2. Repetition. The ad says a name or slogan over and over.

3. Social appeal. The ad suggests that if you use a certain product, you will be nice looking and have a lot of friends.

4. Humor. People like and remember things that are funny.

5. Music. People remember short tunes and jingles.

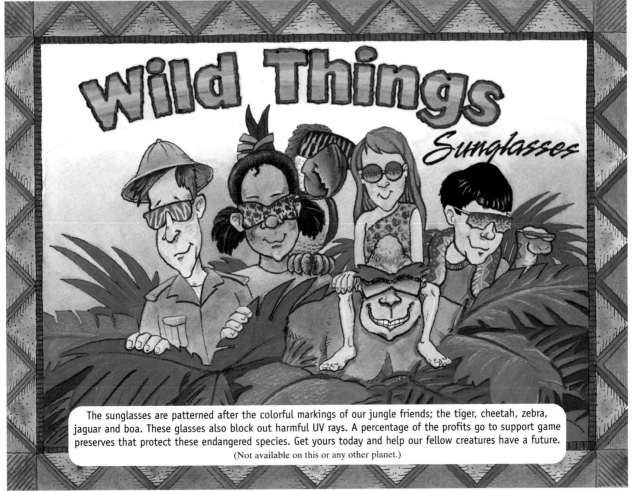

The sunglasses are patterned after the colorful markings of our jungle friends; the tiger, cheetah, zebra, jaguar and boa. These glasses also block out harmful UV rays. A percentage of the profits go to support game preserves that protect these endangered species. Get yours today and help our fellow creatures have a future.

(Not available on this or any other planet.)

What does the ad try to get you to believe about wearing Wild Things Sunglasses?

Economics in Early Utah

Today, Utah businesses use the free enterprise system, like businesses do everywhere else in the United States. However, a system of free enterprise did not always exist here.

At first, American Indians worked together to help the whole group and not just themselves. They cooperated. They did not buy and sell land. They hunted together and found places where the whole group could live. They shared the food they found or grew. By sharing and helping each other, they could all do better than if they worked alone.

When the first pioneers came to Utah, they had an economic system based on need instead of profit. Brigham Young said that the forests and land and water and minerals belonged to all the people. So, at first, people were given land to farm and live on. They did not have to buy it. No one could buy land and sell it at a higher price to make a profit.

The early settlers here started buying and selling with the forty-niners and the soldiers who came here. We have already talked about the stores that soon opened up. Utah's economic system was soon much like that in other places in the U.S.

In early Utah, many jobs were provided to immigrants by the Mormon church. These men worked cutting granite in the canyons. Other men then hauled it down to build the Salt Lake City Mormon Temple.

Immigrants Become Entrepreneurs

After the railroad came, more and more other people came to Utah, as well as to other parts of the United States. It was now much easier for immigrants to travel to find jobs and new homes. They came from Eastern and Southern Europe, from Asia, from the Middle East, and from Mexico. They were Russian, Polish, Hungarian, Serbian, Slavic, Greek, and Italian. They were Japanese and Chinese. They were Armenian and Persian and Mexican.

Most immigrants got jobs working for other people when they came to this country. The pay was usually very low. If they did not know the language, the men and women had to do jobs no one else wanted. Even doctors, university professors, or skilled furniture makers in the "old country" might end up cleaning floors, laying railroad track, or working in mines in America. It was not a good way to live.

People wanted better work. Thousands of immigrants became **entrepreneurs**. An entrepreneur is someone who has an idea and the courage to start a business. Entrepreneurs work for themselves. Usually the whole family helped with the business. Even the children sanded, sewed, hammered, chopped, ran errands, or whatever needed to be done. When the business grew, the family hired other employees.

This entrepreneur had his own business. He traveled from home to home, sharpening scissors and knives.

Utah Entrepreneurs

Kuniko Teresawa arrived in Utah in 1914 with her husband, Uneo. They attended Salt Lake's Buddhist Temple. They started a Japanese language newspaper in Salt Lake City to tell other Japanese immigrants what was happening back home in Japan. The paper was called the *Utah Nippo*. When Uneo died Kuniko kept publishing it until she was more than ninety years old.

Nippo means daily in Japanese. At first the paper came out every day, then every other day, then every week, and finally once a month. But Kuniko did not change its name. She said that she still worked on it every day, no matter how often it came out.

"My food will taste especially good tonight because I have worked hard today," Kuniko told her daughter Kazuko, who helped her. "Tomorrow will be another long day, but that is good. Life is kind to those who work hard and are humble."

She lived in Utah for more than eighty years, but she never learned to speak English. She knew only one English sentence: "That is a cat."

JAN. 22 1909

People made money by working for someone else, or by opening their own business. This is a butcher shop business in 1909.

Immigrants often used skills they already knew before they came here. This man from Germany is making furniture to sell.

Many immigrants began their businesses with a skill they had learned in their old country. Perhaps an Italian baker opened his own bakery here. Perhaps a tailor from Greece opened her own clothing store. People who made furniture in Germany could make furniture here, and sell it themselves. They could also hire other people to work with them. Together they could make more tables, chairs, and cupboards. Together they could have a good business.

Some entrepreneurs sold goods. Maybe they made hats and sold them. Maybe they made rugs, tables, or wagons. Maybe they farmed and sold the wheat, potatoes, or apples.

Some entrepreneurs sold services. They may have delivered groceries, painted homes, or taught classes. They may have opened their own barbershops and cut hair.

Factors of Production

There are four things that must come together before something is sold as a good or service. These things are called factors of production. Factors of production are: land, labor, capital, and entrepreneurship. Let's see what these things mean:

Land (natural resources): People use the term "land" to mean anything that is found in nature. If you are making chairs, the natural resource might be wood. It is from the land. If you are making a teddy bear and need cotton to stuff the bear, you are using a natural resource because cotton grows on the land.

Labor: To provide goods and services, there must be labor. Labor means the work that people do. Even if you bought a robot, it took labor to make it. There is the person who built it, and the person who sold it. Carpenters, teachers, sales people, lawyers, secretaries, actors, race car drivers, and baseball players all do labor.

Capital Goods: When you use something that is already made to make something else, you are using a capital good. The hammer and nails a carpenter uses are capital goods. The paint, canvas, and brushes an artist uses are capital goods. In business, the money you need to run the business is also called "capital."

Entrepreneurship: This means owning and running a business. It often starts with an idea. The person must be willing to take a risk to make the idea work. Entrepreneurs use the land, labor, and capital goods to make money.

Activity
Factors of Production and Sugar Beets

Did you know that for many years Utah farmers provided sugar? They plowed the fields, planted the sugar beets, and weeded, watered, and thinned them as they grew. After the harvest they cooked the beets, mashed them, and got a sweet syrup from them. They dried the syrup into sugar crystals. Then the sugar was packed into bags and shipped to places in Utah and other states. It was hard work to produce sugar!

What factors of production were needed by the sugar beet industry?

Activity
Ideas for Young Entrepreneurs

Adults aren't the only people who become entrepreneurs. Kids can, too. Danyelle Lowers, a 4th grader, started a video rental business from her own collection of tapes. She typed a list and delivered a flyer to nearby homes. She delivers and picks up videos on her bike after school.

Is she selling goods or a service?

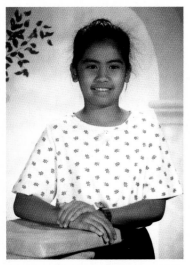

Danyelle Lowers rents her own videos to neighbors.

What business could you start? Will you provide a good or a service? What sounds like more fun to you? Choose something you like. That is very important. You are more likely to stay with something you enjoy. Here are some ideas to help get you started.

Service Suggestions:

■ **House Watcher**

While people are away on vacation, offer to get their mail, turn on lights, and water their plants.

■ **Dog Walker**

Many dog owners don't get home from work until late. Offer your service after school and on weekends.

■ **Garbage Can Service**

Offer to take cans out to the street on collection day and return them to the garage after school.

■ **Lawn Mower**

Ask your family and your neighbors if you can mow their lawn. Always do it at the same time every week. Ask them where they want you to put the grass.

■ **Photograph Organizer**

Take people's boxes and envelopes of pictures and put them in photo albums for them. (Grown-ups hate that job!)

Problems at Work

When people in Utah started working in mines, factories, and businesses, there were many problems for workers. These problems were the same as in other places in the country.

When Utah became a state more than 3,000 children under age sixteen worked in mines and factories. Instead of being in school, they were wage earners. Children as young as ten worked and did not often go to school. Their families needed the money they made. Companies hired children because they didn't have to pay them very much.

More than 18,000 women worked outside their homes for wages. They worked because their families needed the money. They worked long hours, six days a week, and got only Sunday off. Their pay was much lower than the pay men got, even if they worked at the same jobs.

Women ironed shirts to provide money for their families. The man was the owner of the business.

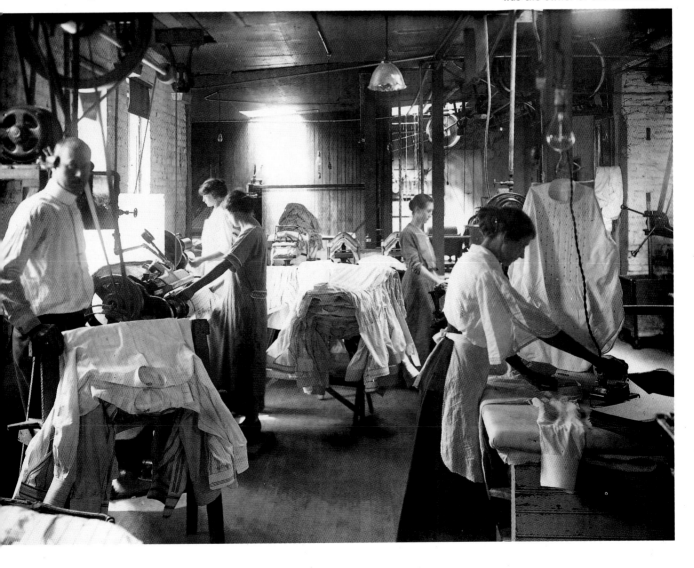

Cutting ice on Utah Lake in 1892 could be dangerous. If the men got hurt, the company didn't have to pay them while they could not work. Later new laws protected workers.

Sometimes companies did not care about the health or safety of their employees. Many places were unsafe to work in. Mines were especially dangerous. There were many mine explosions and accidents. People who got hurt at their jobs couldn't work anymore. So they received no pay from the company. Even though they got no pay, they still needed money to pay the doctor and feed their families. It was a terrible problem.

Sometimes a company went out of business, and the workers lost their jobs. They received no money to help them until they could get another job.

If older workers were ready to retire, they did not receive any retirement pay from the company. They had no way of getting money they needed unless they had been able to save it.

Laws to Protect Workers

Here are some of the things the Utah Legislature tried to do about these problems. It did these things after people wrote them letters and talked to them and told them what the problems were and what needed to be done.

In 1902 it passed a law setting up mine safety rules. A law in 1911 said that children under fourteen could not work in unsafe jobs. Children could not work at night. They could not work for more than fifty-four hours a week. (Today most men and women work only forty hours a week.)

Other laws said that women could not work at jobs outside the home for more than nine hours a day. (Today, most people work eight hours a day.) Another law said women had to be paid at least $1.25 a day at their jobs.

Another law arranged for payments for people who were hurt on the job.

As the years went by, government all over the United States, as well as in Utah, tried to make sure that businesses followed certain other laws. Here are a few of them:

- Today companies are not supposed to say anything about their product that is not true. They have to put labels on packages to tell exactly what is in foods.
- Businesses have to pay at least a minimum wage to their workers.
- Young children cannot work in most jobs. Children now have to go to school instead of to work.
- Men and women of all races have to be paid the same.

- People with physical disabilities cannot be refused jobs just because they have a disability.
- Factories must have good lighting and safe working conditions.

Labor Unions

Another way people tried to solve problems was with **labor unions**. Labor unions are groups of workers. They join together to try to make work places better.

A hundred years ago, workers' days were long and hard. A miner could work all day down under the ground and still barely make enough money to feed his children. If workers complained, they were fired.

Today most people work just forty hours a week. They receive extra pay for working overtime. Many companies buy insurance for their workers, too. Insurance helps pay for doctors and hospitals if the worker's family gets sick. These things have been brought about mostly by the work of labor unions.

Unions try to make things better by talking to the company owners. A team of workers together has a better chance to win changes than one person alone does. They bargain with the bosses about working hours, pay, vacations, sick leave, and safety rules. If the boss won't change things, the workers may go on strike and stop working until they get some of the things they want.

Railroad workers, miners, and carpenters were some of the first workers in Utah to form unions. Now many different kinds of workers belong to unions. Sales clerks and plumbers belong. Musicians who made the CDs you like belong to their own union. Your teachers probably belong to a union.

> **"Together we can do things we can't do alone."**
>
> —*Industrial Workers of the World*

Utah mine workers joined labor unions to get their bosses to give them better pay and safer working conditions.

The Utah Adventure!

This book is a good example of how free enterprise economics works. Utah's students needed a new Utah history book. A company decided to produce the book. The owner of the company hired people to work on the book. Everyone wanted it to be a book children would really like. They worked hard to make it interesting and tell a true story of Utah. They also hoped the teachers would like the book enough to buy it, so the company would make a profit.

It took the services and products of many people in different parts of the world to make the book. Here is what happened:

The author in Salt Lake City, Utah studied about Utah's history. He went to libraries and read books about Utah. He read the diaries of people who had lived here a long time ago. He typed the words on a computer. The editor was in charge of making sure the spelling and punctuation were right. She found the photographs. She hired an artist to paint some of the pictures. A different artist who lives in Minnesota used a computer to arrange the words and pictures on each page. She chose a photo to put on the cover. All of these things took over a year to do.

Making a book is an adventure! It is part of the economics of Utah and other places in the world.

When the book was ready to be printed, it was sent across the Pacific Ocean to Singapore. The paper came from trees in Asia. Someone made and sold the ink to the printer. Many workers there printed the book on huge presses. They used machines to sew the pages together and glue the covers on. After about four months the books were brought to America on a ship. The ship landed in San Francisco. Then large boxes of books were brought to Utah in trucks.

All of the people who worked on the book had to be paid for their services. All of the machines, computers, paper and even ink had to be paid for. Where did the money come from?

You and your friends are the consumers. Your school paid for your books. The schools got the money from the government. The government got the money from taxes. The taxes were paid by the adults in your town. The people earned the money to pay their taxes from their jobs or businesses.

So there you have it. People work hard to provide the goods and services other people need. The work makes them feel good about themselves. It provides money for the workers' families. The work helps provide for the needs of everyone.

What Do You Think?

Do these things with your class.

1. Choose different businesses you know about. What factors of production do you think you will need for each of them?

2. Talk about the differences in working for someone else for money, or starting your own business to make money. What things do you like, or not like, about both ways to earn money?

3. In some countries, there is no free enterprise system. The government owns the businesses, or part of the businesses. Talk with your teacher and parents about some good and bad things about different economic systems.

Can You Remember?

1. In a free enterprise system, who owns the business?

2. Who helps the owner of the business?

3. How do businesses make money?

4. Describe two ways advertisers try to get you to buy.

5. How is an entrepreneur different from an employee?

6. What are the factors of production?

7. What are two problems workers had before government made rules for businesses?

8. Name two things labor unions worked for.

Geography Tie-in

1. Make a list of ten products you or your family own. Then look at labels or wrappers from those products and write the names of the countries they came from. How many countries did you find?

2. As a team, choose a product such as a candy bar, shirt, or even this book. See if you can learn about all of the places where the capital goods (materials) came from, and where the product was made. Make a map showing the route used to bring this product to your home.

Words to Know

capitalistic	goods
consumer	labor union
economic system	product
economics	profit
employee	salary
entrepreneur	service
free enterprise	wage

Glossary

This glossary will help you understand the meanings of the **Words to Know** in this book. They are in **bold type** where they first appear in the book.

abate: to become less in amount; decrease

adobe: a mixture of earth, water, and straw shaped into bricks and hardened in the sun

Anglo: a white person in the United States; people whose native language is English

archaeologist: a scientist who learns about ancient people by studying the things they left behind

artifact: an object used by people long ago

asphalt: mixture of tar and gravel, used to pave roads

atlatl: a spear thrower

barren: land where very few plants live

basin: a low, flat land area shaped like a bowl

bill: a written idea for a new law

budget: a plan for how much money will be needed for expenses

capitalism: where people, not the government, own the land and wealth; Businesses compete with each other to make a profit

capitol: the building where people in the government work

colonize: to settle a new place, but be ruled by another government

communication: being in touch with other people by mail, telephone, etc.

consumer: a person who buys and uses things

constitution: the written rights and laws of a group

continent: one of the seven large land areas of the world

convert: (v) to change another person's beliefs

cooperate: to work together

culture: the way of life of a group of people—their food, clothing, houses, music, religion

diary: a daily written record of personal activities and feelings

democracy: government in which the people hold the ruling power

desert: (v) to leave, as to desert the army, or to desert a city

destructive: harmful

discrimination: treating people unjustly because they are different

diverse: differing from one another

economic system: a way of making and selling goods and services

economics: how goods and services are made, distributed, and used

employee: a person who works for wages

entrepreneur: a person who organizes, manages, and assumes the risk of a business

erosion: wearing away of the land by wind or water

ethnic: people with common traits and customs; belonging to a certain race

Euro-American: an American whose ancestors came from Europe

excavate: to dig up old things

expedition: a trip for the purpose of learning about a new place

extinct: said of a volcano that will never erupt again; said of animals or plants that no longer exist

fossil: the print or remains of a plant or animal

free enterprise: a system where the people run businesses for profit, and where people buy and sell

geography: the study of the Earth and the people, animals, and plants living on it

glacier: a large mass of snow and ice

goods: products that are made, bought and sold

harmony: a feeling of peace and togetherness

historian: a person who studies the past

hogan: a Navajo home, made of logs and earth

immigrant: a person who moves from another country

import: to bring goods into a country

independent: not under another's control

indigenous: plants or animals natural to an area, not brought in from somewhere else

industry: factories and businesses

interpret: to explain

irrigation: a way of supplying water to dry land through ditches, canals, or pipes

isolate: to put all alone

issue: a subject important enough to discuss

kiva: an underground ceremonial room built by the Anasazi people

labor union: a group of workers who join together to bargain for wages and fair treatment

legend: a story passed down through the ages

local: near home

minerals: elements found in the Earth—such as metals, oil, coal, or salt

missionary: a person who tries to convert people to a religion

mosaic: different things put together to make a picture

myth: a story that may not be true but that is important to people

nomad: a person who moves from place to place

ore: rock containing minerals

paleontologist: a scientist who studies dinosaurs

pardon: power to forgive a criminal

permanent: something that lasts a very long time

petrified: plants or animals that turn into rock

pit house: a home of logs and dirt, built partly below and partly above the ground

plateau: a high, wide, flat land area

porter: an attendant on a train; a person who carries baggage

poverty: lack of money for needs

product: something made by manufacture, thought, or growth

prohibit: to ban or forbid

profit: the money made after expenses are paid

racist: the thinking that people in one race are superior to others

rebel: (v) to go against leaders or government

rendezvous: a big fair where trappers sold their furs

representative: a person elected to vote for other people

reservation: an area of land where the U.S. government forced American Indians to live

route: a course of travel

rural: country or farmland; not in a city

service: something done for another person

salary: money paid to an employee

saturate: to soak or fill full

sediment: the material (such as sand and rocks) left behind by water, wind, or a glacier

sedimentary rock: layers of hardened sand and soil built up over thousands of years

self-sufficient: able to provide for needs without outside aid

severe: very harsh, or hard to endure

slang: unusual words used by a group of people

stereotype: to think you know what a person is like, just because that person belongs to a certain group

symbolize: to use an object to mean something else

tepee: an American Indian home, made of tall poles and animal skins

theocracy: government by church leaders

timber: trees cut for wood; logs

tradition: a way of life handed down from parents to children

transcontinental: something that crosses the United States

transportation: moving goods or people from one place to another

unconstitutional: against the rights and rules of the constitution

veto: to reject a bill passed by the legislature

wage: money paid to employees

wagon train: a large group of wagons traveling together

wicki-up: an Indian home, made of branches and brush

Index

Credits

ART

Christensen, C.C.A. 78, 81
Church of Jesus Christ of Latter-day
   Saints Graphics Library 94
Clymer, John 77
Cornell University Press 195
Fairbanks, Avard 91
Fairbanks, J. Leo 85
Hopkinson, Glen S. 87, 89, 113
Jackson, William Henry 70, 96, 146
Price, Clark Kelley 92
Rasmussen, Gary iii, vi, 1, 4, 7, 9, 13,
   16, 18, 19, 27, 28, 29, 31, 36, 46,
   48, 49, 50, 53, 63, 70, 128, 131,
   167, 171, 183, 201
Remington, Frederick 67
Rockwood, Dolly S. 137 (upper)
Salisbury, P. 59, 68
Seivers, Gregory 83, 147 (upper)
Teichert, Minerva 76
Vigos, Jack 107
Weggeland 116, 134

MAPS

Alaine Sweet 5, 6, 8, 11, 14, 16, 32,
   41, 61, 80, 115, 124, 149, 153, 176

PHOTOGRAPHS

Arizona Historical Society 56
Bancroft Library 67 (all), 203
Busath Photography 173 (lower)
Chamberlain, Lynn 3, 10, 17
Church of Jesus Christ of Latter-day
   Saints Archives 84, 119 (all)
Church of Jesus Christ of Latter-day
   Saints Visual Resources 88, 110,
   115, 135 (center), 202, 208
Dinosaur National Park 16 (lower)
George, John 10, 15, 17, 22, 34, 35, 164
Haddon, E.P. 17
Hucko, Bruce 123
Illinois Historical Library 73 (upper),
   135 (upper)
Illinois State Historical Society 183
Jacka, Jerry 40, 47
Jackim, Thomas 10
Joslyn Art Museum 64
Lagoon Corporation 185, 188
Law, Craig 24-25
Los Angeles Public Library 74
Michigan State Archives 200, 204 (lower)
Navajo Nation 44, 51, 122
Nevada Historical Society 29
Ohio Historical Society 191, 192,
   204 (upper)
Oregon Historical Society 86
Ross, Kelly 12
S. George Ellsworth Photographic
   Collection 120, 168, 180
Salt Lake City Historical Society 103
St. Christopher's Mission 55
Teiwes, Helga 16
Till, Tom 2, 13, 15, 33, 144, 153

Union Pacific Railroad 149
University of Utah Libraries 169 (left)
Utah Museum of Natural History
   30 (all), 31 (all), 34
Utah State Governor's Office 173 (upper)
Utah State Historical Society 9, 23,
   39, 42, 43 (all), 45 (upper), 54, 59,
   60, 65, 66, 69, 73 (lower), 79, 82, 98,
   99, 101 (all), 102 (all), 104, 112 (all),
   117, 118, 121, 125, 126, 130, 132,
   135 (lower), 136, 137 (lower), 138,
   140, 141, 142, 147 (lower), 148, 150,
   152, 154, 155 (all), 156 (all), 157,
   158 (lower), 159, 160, 161, 165, 166,
   167, 169 (right), 170, 175 (inset), 178,
   179, 181 (all), 182, 184 (all), 187,
   189 (all), 193, 194, 195, 198, 199 (all),
   205
Ute Tribal Council 50
Wilcox, Bill 175
Wyoming State Archives 38, 45 (lower),
   207, 209
Young, Jeannie 8, 26, 52

All photographs not listed are from the
collection of Gibbs Smith, Publisher.